SAINT JOHN *the* BAPTIST

SAINT JOHN *the* BAPTIST

Priest, Prophet, and Martyr

FR. SEBASTIAN WALSHE, O.PRAEM.

TAN Books
Gastonia, North Carolina

Saint John the Baptist: Priest, Prophet, and Martyr © 2025 Norbertine Fathers of Orange, Inc

All rights reserved. With the exception of short excerpts used in critical review, no part of this work may be reproduced, transmitted, or stored in any form whatsoever, without the prior written permission of the publisher. Creation, exploitation, and distribution of any unauthorized editions of this work, in any format in existence now or in the future—including but not limited to text, audio, and video—is prohibited without the prior written permission of the publisher.

Unless otherwise noted, Scripture quotations are from the Revised Standard Version of the Bible—Second Catholic Edition (Ignatius Edition), copyright © 2006 National Council of the Churches of Christ in the United States of America. Used by permission. All rights reserved.

Excerpts from the English translation of the *Catechism of the Catholic Church*, Second Edition, © 1994, 1997, 2000 by Libreria Editrice Vaticana–United States Catholic Conference, Washington, D.C. All rights reserved.

Cover design by Jordan Avery
Cover image: *St. John the Baptist in the Wilderness* by Philippe de Champaigne (1602–1674). Oil on canvas (c. 17th century). Photo © Lylho / Bridgeman Images.

Library of Congress Control Number: 2024946204

ISBN: 978-1-5051-3141-3
Kindle ISBN: 978-1-5051-3142-0
ePUB ISBN: 978-1-5051-3143-7

Published in the United States by
TAN Books
PO Box 269
Gastonia, NC 28053
www.TANBooks.com
Printed in the United States of America

Contents

Preface . . . . *vii*
Prologue: A Man Named John Was Sent by God . . . . *ix*
Introduction: The World into Which
   St. John the Baptist Was Born 1
Chapter 1: The Birth of John the Baptist 9
Chapter 2: In the Beginning Was the Voice 26
Chapter 3: If You Will Accept It, He Is Elijah 34
Chapter 4: More than a Prophet 47
Chapter 5: Behold, I Send My Angel 61
Chapter 6: John the High Priest 73
Chapter 7: Friend of the Bridegroom 95
Chapter 8: Martyr for Marriage 103

Epilogue: That All Might Believe through Him *114*
Appendix A: Early Christian Writers on John the Baptist *118*
Appendix B: Litany of St. John the Baptist *135*

Preface

The first church in the history of the Order of Praemontre, the order to which I belong, was dedicated to St. John the Baptist. This was not by accident. The chapel was the hub of a fledgling community dedicated to the reform of the clerical life in the Church. And it was a solitary chapel in the wilderness. The figure of St. John, the priest, preaching repentance and crying out in the wilderness to prepare the way of the Lord perfectly encapsulated the vision St. Norbert had for his new community. The Norbertine Order was supposed to be for the Church of the twelfth century what St. John had been for God's people in his own time.

In our own time, the priesthood is in crisis, yet we have no lack of heavenly intercession and protection. May St. John the Baptist once more turn the hearts of the fathers to their children so that the priesthood of Jesus Christ may flourish once again, pure and beautiful, in the Church and for the salvation of the world.

Prologue

A Man Named John Was Sent by God

The prologue to the Gospel according to John is perhaps the loftiest theology found in all of Sacred Scripture. There, the beloved disciple unfolds the mystery of the Word eternally begotten of the Father, together with His coming into the world He created at the Incarnation. Yet, interwoven into this lofty theological discourse is the story of John the Baptist: "There was a man sent from God, whose name was John."[1] The juxtaposition of the account of the inner life of God with the mission of John the Baptist is so stark that many modern scholars simply assert that the parts about John were later additions which did not belong to the original text. While such assertions ignore the fact that the text the Church has received was inspired by the Holy Spirit, who puts everything in its right place, nevertheless, they give testimony to the strangeness of the interweaving of the story of John the Baptist with the story of the eternal Word. But then again, is it so strange that the story of the Word should be bound up with the story of the voice?

---

[1] Jn 1:6. These words of St. John closely parallel the words of St. Luke: "the angel Gabriel was sent from God" (Lk 1:26).

The fact that the Apostle John thought he could not tell the story of the Word made flesh without including the voice crying out in the wilderness reveals that the Gospel itself cannot be told without John the Baptist. We cannot understand Jesus Christ fully without understanding John. So true was this that one of the prerequisites for becoming an apostle was knowledge of John the Baptist. And as John the Apostle goes on to say in his prologue, God sent John so that all might believe through him. We do well, then, to ponder over the life, the mission, and the person of John the Baptist, for in so doing, we shall understand more fully who Jesus Christ is.

Introduction

The World into Which St. John the Baptist Was Born

The coming into the world of St. John the Baptist was an instance of God exercising His dominion as Lord of history. The Russian novelist and philosopher Leo Tolstoy taught that human affairs and individual men were simply the necessary outcome of historical forces, the outcome of an infinite number of infinitesimal actions, no more free or good than the conclusions of calculus. But Christian revelation teaches, in contrast, that human affairs are ultimately intelligible in light of divine providence, since God governs not only human affairs but every detail of the universe. It would be difficult to find a clearer example of this than the birth of John the Baptist. From all eternity, God foreknew and predestined St. John to prepare the way for the Word of God to enter into creation. St. John was not determined by the world into which he came; rather, he was the one who molded and formed the world according to the light which he bore inside of him from God.

The world into which St. John was born was dark on all sides, and yet John was not overcome by the darkness. He was instead a shining lamp, which dispelled the darkness and began to reform a world that had been deformed by sin. St. John came not as a political reformer: he had no political aspirations; he was not dressed in fine garments, nor did he dwell in royal palaces. When he confronted political figures like King Herod, he did so with a view to their salvation, not political advantage. He did not come as an economic savior. Rather than promising the people bread, he lived on locusts and wild honey. Nor did St. John come as a philosopher. He wrote no works, nor did he found a school, though he did gather disciples and teach them. St. John did not even come as a religious reformer, at least not the kind of religious reformer that people were expecting. He did not come to reorganize the worship in the Temple or to take authority from the Levitical priests. Instead, he lived in the desert, far from the Temple and its sacrifices, and he offered to God a pleasing sacrifice from within his own spirit. And it was there that the people spontaneously came to him to be baptized and to be reformed within their own spirits. John had become a new epicenter, a kind of alternative temple, where the people came to find the God of Israel.

There were about half a million people living in Palestine when John was born (about the population of Vermont today), and about eighteen thousand of these residents were clergy, priests, and Levites. Palestine was effectively under Roman control, though Herod the Great was the acting king. He was allowed to rule without significant interference from the Romans so long as he remained loyal to Rome and stability was maintained in his kingdom. When Herod died a few years after the birth of Jesus, his kingdom was divided into five parts: three of which were non-Jewish lands, and two of which had a significant Jewish population. The Jewish territories were given to two sons of Herod the Great: Herod Archelaus (who ruled Judea, Idumaea, and Samaria) and Herod Antipas (who ruled Galilee and Peraea). However, in AD 6, the Romans deposed Archelaus so that Judea, Idumaea, and Samaria were turned into an imperial province under the control of a Roman prefect. During the public ministry of St. John, the prefect was Pontius Pilate, while Herod Antipas still reigned in Galilee and Peraea. Because the military force given to the prefect was relatively small (about three thousand Roman soldiers), he relied upon local leaders to enforce day-to-day discipline and order so that most of the year, the high priest governed in Jerusalem and mediated between the populace and the prefect. During St. John's public ministry, the high priest Caiaphas was effectively governing Jerusalem and its environs.

Perhaps as a result of the Maccabean revolts, combined with the relative unimportance of the region, Rome thought it prudent not to impose Greco-Roman customs upon the Jewish territories. This was reflected in a series of decrees by Julius Caesar, Augustus Caesar, and the Roman senate. For example, in respect for the Jewish observance of the Sabbath, the Jews were exempted from conscription in the Roman army, nor did Rome colonize Jewish Palestine. So the Jews were allowed to practice their religion largely unmolested. Nevertheless, they knew well that they were politically dependent upon and subject to the Romans so that, at the behest of the Romans, they lived as guests in their own land. Besides the military presence, some persons of gentile origin lived among and mingled with the Jews, though they were not very many. Most of these gentiles living in Jewish territories were natives of nearby gentile cities or of Syrian origin.

The economic condition of the region was poor but not destitute. Some areas of Galilee were even modestly prosperous. The majority of inhabitants were able to support their families and pay their taxes. Most Jews supported themselves through fishing, agriculture, or manual labor, such as building. On the other hand, in this society, even basic healthcare was a luxury rather than a necessity, and only those who were rich could afford to see doctors. The Palestine of John's life was, therefore, abundant with many sick and injured people, as the Gospels frequently attest. Of the few who did become rich, most were merchants who served the Temple or aristocrats who were largely associated with the religious ruling class. Thus, a kind of religious-economic division arose, which lent itself to the narrative that those who were outwardly religiously observant were blessed by God with material prosperity. It was this view which seems to have prompted the apostles to exclaim in surprise, "who then can be saved?" when Jesus asserted that it was exceedingly difficult for the rich to enter into the kingdom of God.[1]

A number of significant sects existed in Jewish Palestine during St. John's lifetime. These sects included the Herodians, the Pharisees, the Sadducees (all mentioned in the New Testament), and the Essenes. Very little is known about the Herodians outside of the information given in the New Testament. There are some indications that they may have considered Herod the Great as a messiah figure and that

---

[1] See Mk 10:25; Mt 19:24; and Lk 18:25.

salvation for Israel would come from the continuation of the Herodian Dynasty. The Pharisees numbered about six thousand men and were reputed to be highly observant of the ceremonial and external precepts of the law. In addition to the Pentateuch (the first five books of the Old Testament ascribed to Moses), the Pharisees accepted a number of precise interpretations of the law based upon theological reflections and disputations by learned commentators. The Sadducees were numerically the smallest sect but politically the most powerful and influential. They included Caiaphas, the high priest, and composed the majority of the Sanhedrin, the Jewish religious council by which Jesus was condemned. Sadducees accepted the Pentateuch but did not accept many of the later theological developments (sometimes called the "traditions of the fathers") which the Pharisees accepted. The most notable theological point of dispute between the Pharisees and the Sadducees concerned the resurrection of the body: a doctrine approved by the Pharisees but rejected by the Sadducees.[2] The Essenes are not directly referenced in the New Testament, but abundant historical evidence indicates that they were active during the lifetime of St. John in significant numbers. It was a community of Essenes who lived at Qumran on the shores of the Dead Sea who preserved a cache of documents now known as the Dead Sea Scrolls. The Essenes had practically separated themselves from mainstream Judaism, and they seem to have considered the priesthood and worship in the Jerusalem Temple to be illegitimate by the beginning of the first century AD.

---

[2] See Acts 23:6–9.

Because St. John lived in the desert away from the Temple worship, some have speculated that he was either a member of this community or somehow influenced by them. But while St. John may have known the Essenes, it is clear that he acted on his own initiative and under a special mandate from God, not as a member of a religious community.

The majority of believing Jews had some kind of hope in a divine intervention which would liberate Israel. There was little agreement, however, about the particular way in which this deliverance would be accomplished. Many believed in a Messiah or Christ, a son of David, who was to come. Some thought that deliverance would come through a great war in which God would intervene in a miraculous way. Others believed that so long as Jews perfectly followed the divine law, God would restore peace, prosperity, and autonomy to Israel without the need for battle. Yet most agreed in hoping for something akin to a political salvation, and perhaps only a few of the most spiritually advanced Jews looked for a moral and spiritual salvation. This diversity of religious sects and beliefs, together with the episodic destruction of their hopes as pretender after pretender came forward claiming to be the messiah only to be unmasked as another deceiver, led to a growing sense of despair among the common Jews.

If this were not enough, Herod the Great was becoming more and more paranoid (a paranoia verging upon mental illness according to some historians). To maintain his grasp upon power, he killed a number of his own family members as well as the male claimants from the old Hasmonean royal line. His campaign of terror was supported by ruthless soldiers and a network of spies so that anyone who might seem to lead a revolt, real or imagined, was systematically killed. Herod's slaughter of the children of Bethlehem was the culmination of his cruel tactics, and it perfectly conforms to the portrait of his character reported by historians of that time.

One might think that the death of Herod would have granted some relief, but the opposite was true. Many thought of his death as an opportunity to establish a free Israel, and so a number of open rebellions arose. As a result, Herod Archelaus, the young son of Herod the Great, sent his entire army to quell the rebellion. Josephus reports that three thousand men belonging to the rebellion were killed as a result of this conflict. Archelaus cancelled the Passover to prevent further uprisings, but the feast of Pentecost proved to be the occasion for further sedition. Consequently, the Romans sought assistance from Varus, the governor of Syria, who invaded Galilee first, including the region near Nazareth, then Judea, with two Roman legions together with allied forces. Josephus reports that two thousand rebels were crucified as a result of the campaign of Varus. And while Roman governance was eventually restored, deep resentment of the civil authorities burned within the hearts of many in Israel, especially those of the newly founded Zealot movement to which Simon the Apostle belonged. This superficial peace, undergirded by an aggrieved populace, remained in place throughout the entire lifetime of St. John and of Jesus and ultimately lead to the catastrophe of the late 60s in which Jerusalem was totally destroyed and the Temple demolished, never to be rebuilt again.

It is, therefore, understandable why any notable religious figures of this time should be suspected also of sedition and insurrection. The great crowds following Jesus provoked just this fear in Caiaphas and the other Jewish leaders.³ St. John seems to have initially avoided this scrutiny by living and ministering in a remote region far from major population centers. Nevertheless, as we shall see, his condemnation of the unlawful marriage of Herod Antipas brought about his own condemnation and death. It was a dangerous thing to be a holy man in ancient Israel.

---

³ See Jn 11:45–50.

Chapter 1

The Birth of John the Baptist

St. Luke alone relates the details of the conception and birth of St. John. He seems to have received much of his information from the Virgin Mary herself, since many of the things recorded in his infancy narrative could have only come from her. Perhaps also he might have interviewed some of Mary's close relatives. However he obtained this knowledge, St. Luke clearly intends to make a comparison between St. John and Jesus. First, he recounts the annunciation and conception of John, followed by the annunciation and conception of Jesus. Then he recounts the birth and circumcision of John with a brief account of his growth, followed immediately by an account of the birth and circumcision of Jesus, with an account of His growth. Finally, St. Luke narrates the beginning of John's public ministry and follows this with an account of the beginnings of Jesus's public ministry. So, given the obvious fact that a comparison is being drawn between them, the question is: What is the reason for this comparison?

Things which are close together are easily confused, and this seems to have been the case with St. John and Jesus: "As the people were in expectation, and all men questioned in their hearts concerning John, whether perhaps he were the

Christ."[4] The shining lamp was mistaken for the Light, the best man for the Bridegroom, the voice for the Word. By placing the divinely ordained elements of John's life side-by-side with the corresponding elements of the life of Christ, St. Luke allows us to see in just what respects John was like Christ and in what respects he was unlike Christ.

The Annunciation of John

St. Luke describes the annunciation of John in Luke 1:5–22. There, the angel Gabriel announces the conception and birth of John to John's father, the priest Zechariah. Zechariah was married to Elizabeth, a daughter of Aaron (as the law required) and the cousin of the Blessed Virgin Mary. The circumstances of the annunciation of John are remarkable. Zechariah was one of many Levitical priests who served in turn in the Temple of the Lord. In fact, the descendants of Aaron, the first high priest, were divided into several groupings. As is recorded in 1 Chronicles 24:1–19, by means of lots, David divided the descendants of Aaron into twenty-four groups, which would take turns exercising the priestly office in the Temple. Of these twenty-four, the eighth was Abija, from which Zechariah was descended. Zechariah was chosen by lot to exercise the ministry of the high priest in the Temple by offering incense at the altar of incense, which stood directly in front of the curtain that veiled the Ark of the Covenant. In his commentary on the Gospel according to Luke, St. Ambrose goes so far as to assert that Zechariah was the acting high priest: "Zechariah seems here to be designated High Priest, because only the

---

[4] Lk 3:15.

High Priest went into the second tabernacle once every year."[5] This assertion is significant since it not only implies that God recognized Zechariah as the legitimate heir to Aaron[6] but also that John, his son, was in fact the one who by right should inherit the office of high priest.

Zechariah goes in to offer incense at the altar of incense, which stood before the veil that covered the Ark of the Covenant. Here at this altar, while acting as high priest, the angel Gabriel appears to Zechariah to announce that his prayers have been heard:

> Do not be afraid, Zechariah, for your prayer is heard, and your wife Elizabeth will bear you a son, and you shall call his name John. And you will have joy and gladness, and many will rejoice at his birth; for he will be great before the Lord, and he shall drink no wine nor strong drink, and he will be filled with the Holy Spirit, even from his mother's womb. And he will turn many of the sons of Israel to the Lord their God, and he will go before him in the spirit and power of Elijah, to turn the hearts of the fathers to the children, and the disobedient to the wisdom of the just, to make ready for the Lord a people prepared.[7]

---

[5] This opinion of St. Ambrose was shared by St. Augustine and St. Bede, and St. Thomas Aquinas asserts that Zechariah was exercising the office of high priest.

[6] Josephus reports that the recognized high priest at that time was Joazarum (*Antiquities*, Bk. 17, ch. 8). It may be, however, that he was a usurper, or descended from a usurper, so that in the eyes of God, it was Zechariah who was the true high priest. For at this time, new people were occupying the office of high priest every year (see Jn 11:49; 18:13).

[7] Lk 1:13–17.

This annunciation proclaims a series of blessings, beginning with blessings private to the family of Zechariah, then one common to their neighbors and kinfolk, and finally a blessing extending to the whole people of Israel.

The blessing for Zechariah and Elizabeth is the long prayed for offspring, a son of their own bodies. Yet, already something of this blessing is beyond their immediate family: the name to be given the child is not Zechariah, as was traditional for that time. Rather, the child would be given an entirely new name not belonging to his family, John (which means grace of God), to signify that John was not merely to be a blessing to one family, or the carrying on of one man's name, but rather, he would carry God's grace into the whole world. Perhaps Zechariah was saddened at hearing that his son would not be named after him. God was calling him to expand his love beyond his own family to all of God's people, to give his son away as a gift to others. Perhaps Zechariah was not yet willing to make this sacrifice. This might be the reason for his defective faith in response to the angel: "And Zechariah said to the angel, 'How shall I know this? For I am an old man, and my wife is advanced in years.' And the angel answered him, 'I am Gabriel, who stand in the presence of God; and I was sent to speak to you, and to bring you this good news. And behold, you will be silent and unable to speak until the day that these things come to pass, because you did not believe my words, which will be fulfilled in their time.'"[8]

---

[8] Lk 1:18–20.

Zechariah did not need another sign. An angel had already miraculously appeared to him in the holiest of places. And so, he who would not listen to the word of truth is made unable to hear. And he who was not worthy of communicating to others the divine revelation he did not believe was made unable to speak. In any case, we know that the moment he assents to the name John, his tongue is loosed and he bursts forth in praise of the Lord, and in complete consent to the Lord's plan to give John to the whole people.

The blessing for their neighbors and kinsfolk was first that they could rejoice that their kinswoman was given a child, and moreover that he would be "great before the Lord," giving honor and glory to his people and place of origin: "Now the time came for Elizabeth to be delivered, and she gave birth to a son. And her neighbors and kinsfolk heard that the Lord had shown great mercy to her, and they rejoiced with her. . . . And all these things were talked about through all the hill country of Judea; and all who heard them laid them up in their hearts, saying, 'What then will this child be?' For the hand of the Lord was with him."[9]

The blessing for the whole people is that this child would be specially consecrated to the Lord and become a great prophet like unto Elijah who would bring about a great conversion in Israel and prepare them for the coming of the Lord. The angel's prophecy about wine and strong drink seems to have a double meaning. For in two places the Lord required that a man abstain from wine and strong drink: in the prescriptions for a Nazarite (Nm 6), which were imposed

---

[9] Lk 1:57–58, 65–66.

upon Sampson (Jgs 13), and in the prescription for the exercise of the office of high priest (Lv 10:9). This indicates that John would in some way be like the high priest, Aaron, and in some way be like the judge Sampson. We have already seen that John's father was exercising the office of the high priest. Later, we shall see that John mysteriously takes on the role of the high priest far from the Temple, yet offering a pleasing sacrifice to the Lord. Moreover, the command that the high priest drink no wine or strong drink was in effect before they entered into the tabernacle so that they could distinguish between the sacred and the profane. But John was given this instruction even from the womb, for from the time the Holy Spirit came upon him in his mother's womb, John would always minister before God in the holy place of his spirit.[10] And just as Sampson began the deliverance of the people of Israel from the Philistines[11] (a deliverance that would be completed by David), both in life and in death, so too John would begin the deliverance of the people from spiritual enemies: the demons and those under their control (a deliverance that would be completed by Christ, the son of David). And he would do this during his life, but especially by his death.[12] And just as Sampson would be consecrated to God from his mother's womb, so also John would be sanctified by the Holy Spirit in his mother's womb.

---

[10] See Jn 4:23.
[11] See Jgs 13:5.
[12] Interestingly, Herod Antipas, the tetrarch who had John beheaded, was descended from Edomites, and many Jews did not consider him to be authentically Jewish. So in some way, there is a likeness between the conflict between Sampson and the lords of the Philistines and the conflict between John the Baptist and Herod.

The sanctification of John in his mother's womb calls to mind another prophet whose life in many ways prefigures the life of John: the prophet Jeremiah. At the beginning of his call, the Lord says to Jeremiah: "Before I formed you in the womb I knew you, and before you were born I consecrated you; I appointed you a prophet to the nations."[13] The Lord goes on to say: "Behold, I make you this day a fortified city, an iron pillar, and bronze walls, against the whole land, against the kings of Judah, its princes, its priests, and the people of the land. They will fight against you; but they shall not prevail against you, for I am with you, says the Lord, to deliver you."[14] The fortitude and unyielding integrity required by the prophet Jeremiah was also required of St. John. John would have to act upon and reform the people, not be formed or influenced by them. This explains why even before birth, he would have to be confirmed in God's grace, which impelled him to live in the wilderness apart from men from a very early age. John's message and ministry were not a mixture of human teachings or motives with divine ones. He was wholly dedicated and consecrated to the Lord as a perfect and pure instrument of divine teaching.

John's sanctification in his mother's womb is fulfilled in short order at the time of Mary's visitation. This remarkable event takes place in the peaceful hill country of Judea, far from the hustle and bustle of Jerusalem—a place of quiet, fresh air, and beautiful pine trees. Today, the church of the Visitation stands over the place where the home of Zechariah

---

[13] Jer 1:5.
[14] Jer 1:18–19.

and Elizabeth once stood. It is one of the jewels of the Holy Land where, still today, a profound sense of grace and peace endures, as if Mary's "shalom" forever rests upon that place. Here is St. Luke's account:

> In those days Mary arose and went with haste into the hill country, to a city of Judah, and she entered the house of Zechariah and greeted Elizabeth. And when Elizabeth heard the greeting of Mary, the babe leaped in her womb; and Elizabeth was filled with the Holy Spirit and she exclaimed with a loud cry, "Blessed are you among women, and blessed is the fruit of your womb! And why is this granted me, that the mother of my Lord should come to me? For behold, when the voice of your greeting came to my ears, the babe in my womb leaped for joy. And blessed is she who believed that there would be a fulfilment of what was spoken to her from the Lord."[15]

The word of the Virgin Mary corresponds exactly with the moment that John leaps in his mother's womb and Elizabeth is filled with the Holy Spirit. This is no mere coincidence of timing, as if it just so happens that the infant John leaps for joy when his mother hears the Virgin Mary's greeting. In fact, St. Luke has carefully indicated that it is precisely this word of the Virgin Mary which *causes* both John and his mother to be filled with the Holy Spirit. St. Luke has recorded a number of striking parallels between the life of the Virgin Mary and Zechariah, the father of John the Baptist. There is

---

[15] Lk 1:39–45.

an annunciation to Zechariah followed by an annunciation to Mary (both by Gabriel). Both Zechariah and Mary ask a question. Both receive an answer, which includes a sign about Elizabeth conceiving. Both go to Zechariah's house to visit Elizabeth. Both end with a canticle of praise to God. Those are five parallels. So it is obvious that St. Luke wants us to compare Mary and Zechariah. There are obvious similarities, but also significant differences. Zechariah's question is one of doubt, Mary's question, while superficially like Zechariah's, is actually a question prompted by faith. She asks not whether the angel's word will be accomplished but how. Zechariah's sign is a punishment to help bring about faith, Mary's sign is a reward for faith. This leads us to the event of the Visitation.

St. Luke tells us that Zechariah "went to his home" and "after these days his wife Elizabeth conceived, and for five months she hid herself."[16] When Zechariah comes to Elizabeth, he conceives John in a carnal way, by carnal means. But when Mary comes to Elizabeth, what happens? At Mary's word, Elizabeth is "filled with the Holy Spirit" and the infant John "leaped for joy." This is the fulfillment of the word of the angel concerning John: "he will be filled with the Holy Spirit, even from his mother's womb." The analogy between Zechariah and Mary is striking: when Mary speaks, Elizabeth and John are filled with the Holy Spirit, with divine life. Just as Zechariah is an instrument in causing natural life, Mary is an instrument in causing supernatural life. In other words, Mary is revealed to be a mediatrix

---

[16] Lk 1:23–24.

of grace—that is, of divine life in souls. And if Mary's word is somehow instrumental in the grace given to Elizabeth and John at the Visitation, it is not difficult to look back at Mary's word at the moment of the Incarnation to see how Mary becomes even an instrument to bring about the grace of the Incarnation itself. God made the Incarnation, the source of all other graces, depend upon Mary's word of consent.

Let us return to the final words of the prophecy of the angel Gabriel to Zechariah: "And he will turn many of the sons of Israel to the Lord their God, and he will go before him in the spirit and power of Elijah, to turn the hearts of the fathers to the children, and the disobedient to the wisdom of the just, to make ready for the Lord a people prepared." This conversion of the sons of Israel to God their Father is simultaneous with the conversion of the "hearts of the fathers to their children and the disobedient to the wisdom of the just." This last phrase is a citation of the fourth chapter of the prophet Malachi who prophesies: "Behold, I will send you Elijah the prophet before the great and terrible day of the Lord comes. And he will turn the hearts of fathers to their children and the hearts of children to their fathers."[17] The angel Gabriel explains that the turning of the hearts of the children to their fathers means the turning of the hearts of the disobedient (the children) to the wisdom of the just (their fathers). So it is not just a matter of children imitating their fathers even if they encourage wickedness in their sons, but of those who are disobedient hearkening to the wise counsels of those who are just. In other words,

---

[17] Mal 4:5–6.

the turning of the sons of Israel to God their Father is prepared by the restoration of right relationships within their own families. Just and prudent fathers and obedient children living in mutual love and honor is a prerequisite for us to be in a right relationship with God. And while we do not have a record of most of what John taught on the banks of the Jordan, we do know that ultimately, he gave his life in witness to the sanctity of marriage and family. The disordered relationships among Herod, Herodias, and her daughter, incestuous at every turn, was symptomatic of familial love turned into mere lust and self-serving desires. It is likely, therefore, the St. John taught often about the right relationships among family members when urging the people to repent of their sins.

The Annunciation of John Compared with the Annunciation of Jesus

As I mentioned at the beginning of this section, St. Luke wants us to compare Jesus and St. John to see how they are similar and how they differ. Let us now compare the annunciation and conception of John with the corresponding elements in the life of Jesus.

There are many similarities between John and Jesus. As mentioned, it is the same angel Gabriel who is sent to announce the conception and birth of Jesus. This not only assures us that the annunciations are divinely authorized but also that both are of the highest importance, since one of the greatest angels, Gabriel, "who stands before God," is sent as God's emissary in both cases. In both cases, a great son is promised by means of a miraculous conception. In both cases, the child is to be holy already from his mother's womb. In both cases, the one to whom the annunciation was made asks a question. These similarities assure us that John is very much like Jesus, a suitable and worthy herald for the coming of the King, just as the illuminated sky just before the sunrise is a participation in and a preparation for the risen sun. They also teach us that both the life of John and the life of Jesus arise entirely from the divine initiative. Both John and Jesus are sent from the beginning by God into the world, and the world does not form them but instead is reformed by them. Even the doubt of John's father, Zechariah, is unable to prevent God from bringing about all that He wills in regard to John.

But there are also many differences. John was to be "great before the Lord," Jesus was to be "great," not as one who goes before the Lord but rather as the "Son of the Most High." St. Ambrose says: "It was said of John that he should be great, but of him indeed as a great man; of Christ, as of the great God."[18] And while John was to be sanctified in his mother's womb, God the Father was to give Jesus "the throne of David His father," since He was not simply "filled with the Holy Spirit" but conceived by the power of the Holy Spirit. John's father asks a question prompted by doubt, while Jesus's mother asks a question prompted by faith. John's mother is filled with the Holy Spirit after John's conception, while Jesus's mother is full of grace before the conception of Jesus. Most importantly, John is conceived by his father

---

[18] *Commentary on Luke.*

Zechariah in a natural manner, but Jesus is conceived supernaturally by the power of the Holy Spirit so that He has no human father. These differences show that John comes not as the Christ but as one preparing the way for Christ. John is at the end of a period of waiting and promise, a period of symbolic foreshadowing, while Jesus commences a new age of fulfillment and reality: "The law and the prophets were until John."

The Birth and Circumcision of John

The Virgin Mary seems to have remained with Elizabeth up until the time of John's birth. St. Luke does not directly say whether she left before or after John was born. And our own sentiments incline us to believe that our Lady would have stayed to assist her cousin with the birth. Why leave right beforehand when she seems to have come for the purpose of assisting her cousin? But if she did, St. Luke does not record any role she played in John's birth. So perhaps the Virgin Mary was moved by the Holy Spirit for reasons beyond ordinary human considerations to leave right before the birth of John. In any case, John's birth takes place, just as the angel Gabriel had prophesied:

> Now the time came for Elizabeth to be delivered, and she gave birth to a son. And her neighbors and kinsfolk heard that the Lord had shown great mercy to her, and they rejoiced with her. And on the eighth day they came to circumcise the child; and they would have named him Zechariah after his father, but his mother said, "Not so; he shall be called John." And they said

to her, "None of your kindred is called by this name." And they made signs to his father, inquiring what he would have him called. And he asked for a writing tablet, and wrote, "His name is John." And they all marveled. And immediately his mouth was opened and his tongue loosed, and he spoke, blessing God.[19]

Already many of the things which the angel foretold took place: the child is filled with the Holy Spirit from his mother's womb; the child born is a son; his birth is a cause of rejoicing for many; and Zechariah names him John. The naming of the child happens officially at the circumcision, eight days after his birth. And it was so expected that this first son would be named after his father that the relatives of Zechariah and Elizabeth don't even bother asking what the child's name will be! They just start calling him by his father's name. This prompts Elizabeth to interject to correct them, "No! He shall be called John," implying that Elizabeth had also received a revelation about the child's name. One might think that this would be enough for them, but they are so certain that Zechariah wants his son to bear his name that they turn now to the father as if disregarding what Elizabeth has said. An examination of the genealogies of the Old Testament reveal that it was apparently very uncommon for a son to be given the same name as his father. Why were they so certain that the child was supposed to be named Zechariah that they even ignored the direct statement of his mother?[20] Certainly, the father had the right to name his

---

[19] Lk 1:57–64.
[20] The Scriptures give many examples of mothers having the authority

son in the event that the father and mother disagreed, but they had already intended to call him Zechariah before asking the father, as if they already knew. Why would they be acting under the assumption that Elizabeth was not calling her son by the name Zechariah wanted to call him? One explanation for this could be that Zechariah had for a long time expressed to these same relatives his desire to have a son and to name him by his own name. If this is so, it underlines the strong attachment Zechariah had to rearing a son who would be raised according to his own image: one who would be just like his father.

Perhaps hidden in this episode is that the first father whose heart John turns toward his son is his own father, Zechariah. Zechariah would have to learn to let go of his dreams and plans for his son. Indeed, St. Luke recounts John's upbringing in a single verse: "the child grew and became strong in spirit, and he was in the wilderness till the day of his manifestation to Israel."[21] It seems that John was so strongly moved by the Spirit that as soon as he was able, he left home and lived in the wilderness. Zechariah would have to give his son back to God very soon. This interior letting go of his son was what loosened his tongue and opened his ears at the moment Zechariah acknowledges his name is John, the name given by God, not the name desired by Zechariah. And in his canticle of praise, Zechariah acknowledges that John's mission will be wholly determined by God.

---

and taking the initiative to name their sons (e.g., Ex 2:10; Gn 30:24; Lk 1:31).

[21] Lk 1:80.

The Birth of John Compared with the Birth of Jesus

Let us consider now what St. Luke wants to teach us about the birth and circumcision of John in comparison to Jesus. The first thing to notice is that the account of John's birth is very brief while the account of his circumcision is much longer. Conversely, the account of Jesus's birth is quite long while the account of His circumcision is quite brief. The rite of circumcision was part of the Old Law, destined to pass away with Christ, since the reality it prefigured would replace the symbol. And so, since John was at the terminus of the old covenant, it was fitting that his circumcision be recounted in detail, while with Jesus it is treated as something in passing. Conversely, the birth of John is the birth of one who, though sanctified, yet still lies under the penalty of original sin and death, while the birth of Jesus is the birth of one who is life itself and destined to give life to all who believe in Him.

John is born of aged parents to signify that he belongs to an order which is soon to pass away. Jesus is born of a young virgin to signify the beginning of a new creation. The birth of John, rendered wonderful by the old age of his mother, drew the attention of the neighbors and kinsfolk of Elizabeth, for they came together to rejoice with her and to glorify God's mercy toward her. But the birth of Jesus, having been announced by angels and foretold by a star, drew not only those who were near but also those who were far off—namely, the shepherds and the wise men. And this signifies the greater universality which the new priesthood enjoys over the old. For the old priesthood ministered only to those of the house of Israel, who were united by bonds of blood, while the new priesthood ministers to all men.

All of these differences point to the fact that John's entire life and mission was to prepare a way for the Lord Jesus. And once the means has been used to arrive at the end, there is no longer a need for the means: the symbol passes away while the reality endures; the voice falls silent while the word signified by the voice remains in the heart. As John testified about himself, *He must increase, while I must decrease.*

Chapter 2

In the Beginning Was the Voice

All four Evangelists introduce the public ministry of St. John the Baptist with the same text of Isaiah the Prophet: "A voice cries: In the wilderness prepare the way of the LORD, make straight in the desert a highway for our God."[1] Indeed, St. Luke even sees the fulfillment of this prophecy in the events of John's birth. For Zechariah had been mute due to his unbelief and regains his voice only when he indicates that his son is not to be named Zechariah but John, as foretold by the angel. Just as the Holy Spirit had come first to John and then into his mother, so too, when the son who was the Voice was born, the voice of the father was restored.

Why begin by identifying John as a "voice"? It may help to begin by reading the verse from Isaiah in context.

> Comfort, comfort my people, says your God. Speak tenderly to Jerusalem, and cry to her that her warfare is ended, that her iniquity is pardoned, that she has received from the Lord's hand double for all her sins. A voice cries: "In the wilderness prepare the way of the

---

[1] Is 40:3; cf. Mt 3:3; Mk 1:3; Lk 3:4; and Jn 1:23.

> Lord, make straight in the desert a highway for our God. Every valley shall be lifted up, and every mountain and hill be made low; the uneven ground shall become level, and the rough places a plain. And the glory of the Lord shall be revealed, and all flesh shall see it together, for the mouth of the Lord has spoken." A voice says, "Cry!" And I said, "What shall I cry?" All flesh is grass, and all its beauty is like the flower of the field. The grass withers, the flower fades, when the breath of the Lord blows upon it; surely the people is grass. The grass withers, the flower fades; but the word of our God will stand for ever.[2]

The text goes on to speak of the coming of the Lord God as a shepherd for Israel. The context speaks about Jerusalem in a state of sin, warfare, and punishment. But then a voice in the wilderness cries out. The voice promises an end to sin, warfare, and punishment in the form of the coming of the Lord as a Savior and Shepherd. It is a message of exceeding consolation. The tenderness of this voice is striking when we consider how harshly John spoke to the Pharisees and Sadducees.[3] But we must realize how tenderly John must have spoken to sinners who desired to be freed from their sins. The harshness of John toward the Pharisees and Sadducees was really a form of tenderness when understood as an attempt to cause them to truly acknowledge their sinfulness. Sadly, many of them went away accusing him of being possessed by

---

[2] Is 40:1–8.
[3] See Mt 3:7.

a demon. But the multitude of sinners who knew they were sinners heard from John the most consoling words.

Notice the anonymity of the "voice." One expects to read about a prophet, or about some emissary of the Lord, but instead Isaiah speaks only of a voice, not about the one whose voice it is. On the one hand, this reflects the total humility of John, who thinks of himself merely as a voice, something less than substantial, something destined to vibrate the air and then disappear. At the same time, it reveals John as a perfect instrument of the Lord: it is the voice which speaks the very word of the Lord and has no other purpose, as if to say, John was utterly and completely in the service of the Lord. The purpose of the voice is to express the word, and once it has done so, it passes away.

Notice also that the voice cries out twice in this text. First, the voice cries out about preparing a way in the desert for the coming of the Lord by the removal of obstacles. This first cry ends with the assurance that "the mouth of the Lord has spoken." Second, the voice cries out again about the brevity and uncertainty of life in the flesh but concludes "the word of our God will stand forever." So the promise begins with a voice and ends with a word spoken by the mouth of the Lord.

Voice and word are very similar. The voice is the sound we use to express the word we have conceived in our mind and heart. First, we conceive a word, some thought or idea. Then we express this word through a vocal sound, our voice. The voice makes our interior word known to others so that they too can form within themselves the word which began in us. So the word is in some way before the voice (in the one who speaks) and in some way after the voice (in the one who hears). So, too, the Word of God is in some way before John the Voice as enlightening him, providing him with the object of his preaching, and sending him; and in some way after the Voice, inasmuch as John was born and began his public ministry before Jesus and insofar as, through John, the Word who is Jesus Christ was made known to others. Thus, John says: "This was he of whom I said, 'He who comes after me ranks before me, for he was before me.'"[4]

St. Thomas says that John is prophesied as a voice for three reasons: Because the voice goes before the word, as John went before Christ; second, because through the voice the word is known, so also through John's preaching Christ was made known; and third, because the voice without the word does not direct the mind to some one thing, but the whole of John's preaching was directed to Christ.[5]

St. Augustine makes much of this relationship between voice and word. He remarks both on their similarity and distinction. He is worth quoting at length:

> John is the voice, but the Lord is the Word who was in the beginning. John is the voice that lasts for a time; from the beginning Christ is the Word who lives forever. Take away the word, the meaning, and what is the voice? Where there is no understanding, there is only a meaningless sound. The voice without the word strikes the ear but does not build up the heart. However, let us observe what happens when we first seek

---
[4] Jn 1:15.
[5] Cf. *Commentary on Matthew*, ch.3, v.3.

to build up our hearts. When I think about what I am going to say, the word or message is already in my heart. When I want to speak to you, I look for a way to share with your heart what is already in mine. In my search for a way to let this message reach you, so that the word already in my heart may find place also in yours, I use my voice to speak to you. The sound of my voice brings the meaning of the word to you and then passes away. The word which the sound has brought to you is now in your heart, and yet it is still also in mine. When the word has been conveyed to you, does not the sound seem to say: The word ought to grow, and I should diminish? The sound of the voice has made itself heard in the service of the word, and has gone away, as though it were saying: My joy is complete. Let us hold on to the word; we must not lose the word conceived inwardly in our hearts. Do you need proof that the voice passes away but the divine Word remains? Where is John's baptism today? It served its purpose, and it went away. Now it is Christ's baptism that we celebrate. It is in Christ that we all believe; we hope for salvation in him. This is the message the voice cried out. Because it is hard to distinguish word from voice, even John himself was thought to be the Christ. The voice was thought to be the word. But the voice acknowledged what it was, anxious not to give offence to the word. I am not the Christ, he said, nor Elijah, nor the prophet. And the question came: Who are you, then? He replied: I am the voice of one crying in the wilderness: Prepare the way for the Lord. The voice of one crying in the wilderness is the voice of one breaking the silence. Prepare the way for the Lord, he says, as though he were saying: "I speak out in order to lead him into your hearts, but he does not choose to come where I lead him unless you prepare the way for him." What does prepare the way mean, if not "pray well"? What does prepare the way mean, if not "be humble in your thoughts"? We should take our lesson from John the Baptist. He is thought to be the Christ; he declares he is not what they think. He does not take advantage of their mistake to further his own glory. If he had said, "I am the Christ," you can imagine how readily he would have been believed, since they believed he was the Christ even before he spoke. But he did not say it; he acknowledged what he was. He pointed out clearly who he was; he humbled himself. He saw where his salvation lay. He understood that he was a lamp, and his fear was that it might be blown out by the wind of pride.[6]

St. Augustine begins by attending to the differences between the voice and the Word. The Word is eternal, while the voice endures only for a time. Moreover, the whole purpose and worth of the voice is in the service of the Word. Just as a human voice without a corresponding word has no content, but is just a meaningless sound, or as St. Paul says "a resounding gong or a clashing cymbal,"[7] so too, John's life and preaching would have been empty and meaningless

---

[6] *Hom.* 293, 3: PL 1328–29.
[7] 1 Cor 13:1.

without Christ. And just as the voice passes away once it has served its purpose, so too, John's ministry, his baptism, ceased with the coming of Christ.

Nevertheless, just as we sometimes have a hard time distinguishing between the interior word and the exterior voice, so too, the people had a hard time distinguishing between John and the Christ. Thus, the people were wondering if John was the Christ. For how could the way for Christ be prepared by one utterly unlike Him? God sent John to get the people accustomed to Jesus as, for example, the baptism of John got the people accustomed to the baptism which Jesus would later institute. As St. Thomas taught: "The entire teaching and work of John was a preparation for Christ, just as a minister and inferior artist prepares the matter for the form which the principal artist will introduce."[8] Moreover, John prepared the way not only by his teaching but also by his holy life. In his detachment from the desires of the flesh and worldly goods, John showed us how to despise earthly things. In his devotion to Christ and the things of God, John showed us how to cling to heavenly things. In his bravery against Herod and the Pharisees and Sadducees, John prepared us to fight fearlessly against sin and hypocrisy. In his humble estimation of himself as unworthy even to loosen the sandal of the Lord, John prepared us to become like little children who are able to enter the kingdom of heaven.

In spite of the fact that John's whole life and ministry was to prepare the way for the Lord Jesus, to remove all the obstacles before Him, John himself becomes an obstacle

---

[8] *Summa Theologica*, IIIa, q.38, a.3, c.

when Jesus comes to be baptized by John. The Gospel of Matthew records: "Then Jesus came from Galilee to the Jordan to John, to be baptized by him. John would have prevented him, saying, 'I need to be baptized by you, and do you come to me?' But Jesus answered him, 'Let it be so now; for thus it is fitting for us to fulfil all righteousness.' Then he consented."[9]

John's humility causes him to hesitate at the prospect of baptizing Jesus, just as Peter's humility causes him to resist having his feet washed by Jesus.[10] John's baptism was a baptism for sinners. The washing of feet was the work of a slave. Jesus unexpectedly acting as if He were a sinner and a slave takes devout souls off guard. This model of self-emptying is at the foundation of Christian morality. We must do as Jesus did. If Jesus, who was free from sin, was willing to be considered a sinner in order to accomplish the Father's will, how much more must we, who are in fact sinners, be willing to confess our sins to accomplish the Father's will? If Jesus who is the sinless King of kings was willing to act as our servant, how much more should we who are naturally slaves to sin be willing to serve others? John began to understand this at the baptism of Jesus, and from that time forward, the voice would proclaim Jesus as the Lamb of God, the one who would be sacrificed to take away our sins.

---

[9] Mt 3:13–15.
[10] See John 13.

Chapter 3

If You Will Accept It, He Is Elijah

When representatives of the Jewish leaders came to John to inquire about his identity, the dialogue went like this: "'Who are you?' He confessed, he did not deny, but confessed, 'I am not the Christ.' And they asked him, 'What then? Are you Elijah?' He said, 'I am not.' 'Are you the prophet?' And he answered, 'No.' They said to him then, 'Who are you? Let us have an answer for those who sent us. What do you say about yourself?' He said, 'I am the voice of one crying in the wilderness, "Make straight the way of the Lord," as the prophet Isaiah said.'"[1]

John denies that he is the Christ, or Elijah, or the prophet. How are the last two denials of John to be reconciled with the very words of Jesus concerning John: "What did you go out into the wilderness to behold? . . . To see a prophet? Yes, I tell you, and more than a prophet. . . . For all the prophets and the law prophesied until John; and if you are willing to accept it, he is Elijah who is to come."[2] It sometimes happens that two people use the same word with different meanings in mind. For example, when Jesus said to the Jews who were

---

[1] Jn 1:19–23.
[2] Mt 11:7, 9, 13–14.

asking for a sign, "destroy this temple, and I will raise it up in three days," those Jews thought Jesus was talking about the building they were in, while in fact, Jesus was using the word *temple* to refer to His own body.[3] Similarly, John understood that the Jewish leaders were asking if he was the same physical person Elijah who had lived in the Holy Land eight hundred years earlier. To this, he answered "no." And John knew that when they were asking if he was the prophet, they meant the one foretold by Moses, to which John again replied "no." But Jesus was speaking about John as someone typified by Elijah, who lived and preached and acted very much like Elijah did. So too, the angel Gabriel had said about John that he would come in the "spirit and power" of Elijah. And Jesus said that John was both a prophet and more than a prophet, not because John was the one foretold by Moses (that would be Jesus Himself) but because John would be the last of those who came to foretell the coming of the Christ; furthermore, he would usher in this coming and see it not from afar but also witness the fulfillment of what he foresaw and foretold, which is more than any other prophet saw.

The natural question which comes to mind here is: What does it mean to come in the spirit and power of Elijah? To answer that question, we need to examine in more detail the life of Elijah as recorded in the first and second books of Kings.

---

[3] See Jn 2:19–21.

The Life of Elijah

The life of Elijah is told primarily in the first and second books of Kings (from First Kings 17 until Second Kings 2). Elijah appears suddenly upon the scene without introduction, not even an indication of his father's name. Such an abrupt entrance is uncommon with significant biblical persons. Usually, they are introduced with at least a brief lineage. But not so with Elijah: only his place of origin is mentioned. He is from an area east of the Jordan, outside the Promised Land, settled by the tribe of Gad. There is no indication that he is descended from a kingly or priestly ancestor. But we do know the meaning of his name: Elijah means "the Lord is my God." To both Abraham and Moses, God had made a covenant that he would be the God of the descendants of Abraham. Thus, Elijah seems to in some way fulfill this covenant. He appears just when Ahab, king of Israel, has been influenced by Jezebel, his foreign wife, to make the worship of the Baals and of Asherah the official religion in Israel.

The Baals were a number of different gods, primarily weather and sky gods, whose worship was for the sake of producing rain, fertility, and vegetation, while Asherah was a fertility goddess conceived as a kind of wife to the supreme deity in the local pagan pantheon. It is likely that Jezebel promoted the worship of the Baal of Tyre, since she was the daughter of a king of Tyre. Therefore, the prophecy of Elijah that there would be no rain except at his word was in order to show that it was the God of Israel, not the Baals, who had power over weather.

In sacred history, Elijah is the first person who represents God on earth without being a political ruler or a priest. From Moses down to David, the Spirit of God had come upon each ruler of Israel. And each of them had been selected by God Himself. But with Solomon, the divine appointment of a ruler had ceased (Solomon had been appointed by David, not by God, and all of Solomon's successors had come to the throne without being chosen by God). From the time of Solomon, the history of Israel and Judah had been dominated by political rulers who did not speak in God's name. Yes, some had pleased the Lord, but none had been chosen by God to speak to the people in His name. The coming of Elijah changes all of this. In the latter part of the first book of Kings, it is Elijah, not the kings of Israel, who is the central figure. Their story is told only in relation to his. So this marks a new era in the sacred history of God's people, in which the kingdom of God is disassociated with a political kingdom and understood primarily as a kingdom of those faithful to the Lord. Jesus would bring this movement to completion when He testified before Pontius Pilate, "My kingdom is not of this world."[4]

Elijah, therefore, shows that he exercises authority not like any earthly king but as one who has dominion even over nature: "During these years there shall be no dew or rain except at my word."[5] He says "my word," not "God's word," because he knows that God has granted this authority to him: he shares in God's authority as His minister. Once the

---

[4] Jn 18:36.
[5] 1 Kgs 17:1.

drought begins, Elijah moves about secretly from place to place to avoid being found by Ahab and Jezebel. Notice that Elijah does not think that his divinely delegated authority extends to the preservation of his own life: his authority is for the benefit of others, not his own private good. Nevertheless, God miraculously provides food for him while he is in hiding. In a fascinating detail, it is a raven which God commands to bring Elijah meat and bread. Ravens were unclean and an abomination according to the law,[6] so it seems that God provides for Elijah in a way which bypasses the Mosaic Law. He eventually finds refuge with a widow and her son in Zarephath, a town of Sidon on the seacoast north of Tyre. She is from the very region that Jezebel, Ahab's wife, is from. But while Jezebel comes into the Promised Land and leads Ahab away from the Lord, Elijah leaves the Promised Land and enters into gentile territory in order to lead this woman to the Lord. While living with them, God provides bread and oil miraculously for a year for all of them. But at some point, the widow's son falls ill and dies. Elijah brings him into his upper room and raises him from the dead. In contrast, as we shall later see, all of the sons of Ahab die a premature death and the political rule of the kingdom passes to the heir of another. So the relationship of Elijah with this widow is placed in contrast, even opposition to, the relationship of Ahab with Jezebel. The spiritual family of Elijah is contrasted with the carnal and political family of Ahab.

In the third year of the drought, God sends Elijah to confront Ahab. He proposes a test to determine who is a true and

---

[6] Cf. Lv 11:15; Dt 14:14.

who is a false prophet. Four hundred and fifty prophets of Baal and four hundred prophets of Asherah are summoned, and before all the people, a sacrifice is prepared. The prophets of Baal and Asherah fail to call down fire to consume the sacrifice, once again showing that their gods of the sky did not exist. After this, Elijah's brief prayer is answered by God in spectacular fashion, and the entire sacrifice together with the wood, stones, and water are consumed. Upon seeing this, the people turn back to the Lord and assist Elijah in exterminating all the false prophets of Baal and Asherah. Immediately thereafter, Elijah prays for rain, and a great storm arises from the west and inundates the parched land. Here, Elijah turns the hearts of the Israelites back to Yahweh their Father, and Yahweh, in turn, provides rain again for the earth. This moment in the life of Elijah seems to be the basis for the later prophecy of Malachi that Elijah would return again to "turn the hearts of fathers to their children and the hearts of children to their fathers, lest I come and smite the land with a curse."[7]

When these events are reported to Jezebel, she is infuriated and intends to take Elijah's life, but he escapes. After a day's journey into the desert, utterly exhausted, Elijah lays down to sleep under a broom tree and prays for death. But an angel of the Lord comes with bread and water, and strengthened by that food, Elijah walks forty days and nights to Mount Horeb. There, within a cave, the Lord speaks to Elijah and reassures him that God will not abandon him, that the covenant will not be voided, and that God has

---

[7] Mal 4:5.

preserved a remnant of faithful in the land who have not worshipped the Baals. He instructs him to anoint Hazael as king of Aram, Jehu as king of Israel, and Elisha as a prophet to succeed him. On his return, Elijah comes upon Elisha as he is plowing with twelve yoke of oxen. He anoints Elisha as his successor, and Elisha becomes his assistant and spiritual son. It is Elisha who will eventually anoint Jehu and declare that Hazael would become king of Syria.

The next time Elijah confronts Ahab will be the last time. Ahab, prompted again by Jezebel, has Naboth murdered and goes to take possession of his vineyard. But Elijah meets him on the way and declares the Lord's sentence: Ahab shall die as Naboth has, Jezebel's flesh shall be eaten by the dogs, and every male in the line of Ahab shall be cut off. In response, Ahab repents and humbles himself by works of penance so that the Lord determines not to bring the evil upon him in his own lifetime.

Here we see that it is God's representative on earth who bears true authority among God's people. Ahab (and later his son Ahaziah), as well as Jezebel, are subject to the word of Elijah. Through Elijah, God chooses who will be king and who will be a prophet in Israel. The political structures which heretofore have been acknowledged as passing on divine authority to the rulers of God's people are completely overturned.

Elijah travels through Samaria where he intercepts the messengers of Ahaziah, the son of Ahab (not to be confused with Ahaziah, the king of Judah). Ahaziah had fallen and lay wounded. He therefore sent messengers to Baalzebub, the god of Ekron, to ask if he would survive. But Elijah foretells that because he did not seek the God of Israel, he would perish. Ahaziah sends three successive troops of fifty men to take Elijah captive, but Elijah calls down fire from heaven to consume the first two troops of fifty. The captain of the third troop begs for his life, and Elijah spares him and goes with him to Ahaziah to tell him his fate in person. Ahaziah subsequently dies according to the word of the Lord. Later, Jehu would cut off every male in the line of Ahab, bringing the word of the Lord spoken by Elijah to fulfillment.

In his final journey, Elijah travels with his servant Elisha to Bethel, then to Jericho, and finally across the Jordan opposite Jericho. This is the very place where John the Baptist first began to baptize. As they walk along, a flaming chariot comes between them and takes Elijah up into heaven. As Elisha sees the chariot ascend, the mantle falls from Elijah as a sign that Elisha has received a double portion of his spirit, and Elisha takes his mantle and assumes his office as Elijah's successor. Elisha is the first, but not the last, to bear the spirit of Elijah.

The Spirit and Power of Elijah

In many ways, St. John the Baptist seems an unlikely candidate for one who comes in the spirit and power of Elijah. John performs no miracle, while the life of Elijah is filled with miraculous events. Elijah is victorious over the king and queen of Israel, whose threats prove idle against him, and finally, he is assumed alive into heaven. John is imprisoned by Herod, and Herodias has her revenge upon him by instigating John's beheading. Elijah's life is marked by triumph, John's by failure. And yet, the angel Gabriel declares that John came in the spirit and power of Elijah. We need to understand better in what this spirit and power of Elijah consists.

Right away we notice a number of parallels between the life of Elijah and the life of John the Baptist. John the Baptist begins his public ministry in the place where Elijah was taken up, as if to signify that he is Elijah returned. Elijah and John both lived lives of extreme penance and dwelt and were fed in the wilderness. Both were vested in a hairy garment with a leather belt. Moreover, they both confronted a wicked king and queen of Israel. For just as Ahab had been influenced by his wife, Jezebel, to corrupt Israel, so too, Herod the tetrarch had been influenced by his wife, Herodias, to corrupt Israel. And just as Elijah was sent to restore true worship in Israel, so too, John the Baptist was sent to restore true worship to the descendants of Abraham. Elijah destroys the false prophets at a river to bring about the conversion of the people back to the Lord, while John baptizes at a river to destroy their sinful lives and bring the people back to the Lord. So it is clear from these many, distinct likenesses that Elijah is a type of John the Baptist.[8]

Looking back upon the life of Elijah, we notice that the institutional structures of Israel which had been identified as the instruments of divine authority had all defected from the

---

[8] Another type of John the Baptist, which we will not consider here, is Ezekiel the prophet. Like John, Ezekiel is both a priest and a prophet. Like John, Ezekiel ministered and spoke on God's behalf far from the Temple, and like John, Ezekiel was sent to correct the wicked shepherds of Israel.

Lord. The kings of Israel ruled as any other kings of gentile nations and were not chosen by God. The Temple, built by Solomon in such fanfare, was irrelevant as far as the fidelity of the people to God was concerned. Authentic, public worship of the Lord had all but disappeared from Israel. In such times, God called and sent Elijah as the locus of His Spirit and power on earth. What the kings and priests of Israel could not accomplish, Elijah accomplished through God's spirit and power dwelling within him.

At the time of John the Baptist, a similar fate had befallen the chosen people. Herod was ruling at the pleasure of the Romans, and the scribes, Pharisees, and Sadducees were largely corrupt. The high priesthood had fallen into the hands of a few wealthy men who used their office as a means of gaining wealth and power, and the worship at the temple was not pleasing to God. So God chose and sent John the Baptist as the locus of God's Spirit and power in contrast to the institutional monarchy, priesthood, and temple worship. Jesus implies this state of affairs in many places in the Gospels. When forming His apostles, Jesus contrasts how they are to govern with the way those currently in authority were governing: "The kings of the Gentiles exercise lordship over them; and those in authority over them are called benefactors. But not so with you; rather let the greatest among you become as the youngest, and the leader as one who serves."[9] This implies that the rulers in Israel had begun to rule as any other Gentile kings, and Jesus intends to replace them with His apostles who will shepherd rightly. The Gospels

---

[9] Lk 22:25–26.

also imply that the authority of the chief priests had become corrupt: "One day, as he was teaching the people in the temple and preaching the gospel, the chief priests and the scribes with the elders came up and said to him: 'Tell us by what authority you do these things, or who it is that gave you this authority.' He answered them: 'I also will ask you a question; now tell me, was the baptism of John from heaven or from men?'"[10]

Jesus points to John as a new locus of divine authority outside of the Temple and the institutional priesthood. The chief priests and scribes refuse to acknowledge this authority, but it was plain as day to the people, and so they remained silent.

Like Elijah, John had suddenly, and without human influence, come upon the scene. The angel Gabriel had announced his arrival as a matter of fact, not dependent upon the faith of his father, Zechariah. His name would not be chosen by his father but given by God. The divine life would be granted to him from his mother's womb, antecedent to any merits of John. And from his youth, he would be impelled by God's Spirit to live in the desert in complete communion with God. John was untouched by the world; instead, God Himself would be his teacher and formator. To come in the spirit and power of Elijah means to come as a perfect and docile instrument of the divine Spirit and Power. John acted always as God would have him act, and he spoke only what God instructed him to speak.

---

[10] Lk 20:1–4.

And so the spirit and power of Elijah did not consist in miracles, or condemning his enemies to death, or even in preserving his own bodily life. Those miracles and the preservation of Elijah's life, while the lives of his enemies were destroyed, were merely outward signs of God's power at work, not the essence of the spirit and power which Elijah possessed. Indeed, when the time drew near for the coming of the Savior, a more perfect manifestation of this spirit and power was required. For John had to anticipate the passion and death of the Lord. Though John worked no miracle, his very life was a miracle of moral perfection. And though his foes triumphed over his body, his spirit remained firmly rooted in God and in the hope of the resurrection.

John, even more than Elijah, had come to bear witness to a new and better life and kingdom: a life interiorly united with God, a kingdom of an interior union of hearts and minds. This life and kingdom would only come to full fruition after this present life in a renewed and recreated world. Not only were the institutional structures of Israel insufficient instruments of divine truth and grace, even life in this fallen and corrupt world was insufficient. To tell the whole truth, even life in the Garden of Eden would not have been sufficient to embody the whole plan of God and the life to which He calls mankind to live with Him. John anticipated this revelation and Jesus confirmed it when He spoke of His passion as an exodus, and when, even after His resurrection, He remained no longer in this world but ascended to His Father. There Jesus and John invite us to live with them among the angels of God: "They are equal to angels and are sons of God, being sons of the resurrection."[11] John was Elijah and something more. He was a prophet and more than a prophet.

---

[11] Lk 20:36.

Chapter 4

More than a Prophet

Jesus says of John: "Why then did you go out? To see a prophet? Yes, I tell you, and more than a prophet."[1] Jesus simultaneously asserts that John is a prophet, indeed the greatest of the prophets.[2] Yet, He also asserts that John is "more than a prophet." What does this mean? To understand this statement of Jesus, we must first understand better what it means to be a prophet.

What Is a Prophet?

In a general sense, the word *prophet* signifies someone who sees what others cannot: "for he who is now called a prophet was formerly called a seer."[3] More specifically, a prophet is someone who receives supernatural knowledge from God (by way of revelation) and is enabled to communicate this knowledge to those whom God wills. This knowledge may be of future events, of events far away, or of divine truths above the comprehension of the human mind.[4] For example,

---

[1] Mt 11:9; Lk 7:26.
[2] See Lk 7:28.
[3] 1 Sm 9:9.
[4] See *ST*, IIa-IIae, q. 171.

the prophet Jeremiah knew about the eventual fate of Pashhur;[5] the prophet Ezekiel had a vision of the false worship taking place far away at the Temple;[6] and the prophet Isaiah "saw the Lord sitting upon a throne, high and lifted up."[7] In short, a prophet is able to know things proper to God's knowledge, so long as God reveals them to him. Often, a prophet is also given the ability to perform miracles as a testimony to the divine origin of his knowledge.

There is, however, another aspect of prophecy which sometimes goes unnoticed: a prophet knows and speaks of things far distant so that he anticipates but does not himself immediately or fully attain that good he announces. Thus, St. Thomas teaches: "Prophecy is about those things which are far from our knowledge, and as much as something is farther from human knowledge, so much more properly does it pertain to prophecy."[8] And the letter to the Hebrews states: "And all these, though well attested by their faith, did not receive what was promised."[9] It is true that a prophet sometimes eventually obtains what he had foreseen, as when Moses worshipped God on Mount Sinai. Nevertheless, insofar as he is acting as a prophet, he sees it from afar: "I see him, but not now; I behold him, but not nigh: a star shall come forth out of Jacob, and a scepter shall rise out of Israel."[10] This means that a prophet is one who, in some sense,

---

[5] See Jer 20:3.
[6] See Ez 8:16.
[7] Is 6:1.
[8] *ST*, IIa-IIae, q. 171, a. 3, c.
[9] Heb 11:39.
[10] Nm 24:17.

must wait for the fulfillment of what he foresees and foretastes. The clearest case of this may be Moses, the greatest of the Old Testament prophets, to whom God said: "This is the land which I swore to Abraham, to Isaac, and to Jacob, 'I will give it to your descendants.' I have let you see it with your eyes, but you shall not go over there."[11]

In order for a prophet to see things which belong properly to divine knowledge, it is necessary that he be inspired by the Holy Spirit.[12] For "All scripture is inspired by God,"[13] and "no prophecy of scripture is a matter of one's own interpretation, because no prophecy ever came by the impulse of man, but men moved by the Holy Spirit spoke from God."[14] Thus, every prophet is, in a special way, an instrument of the Holy Spirit, as the tongue is the instrument of the one who speaks.

All Prophecy Is Fulfilled in Christ

Because every prophet is an instrument of the Holy Spirit, every prophet shares in the mission of the Spirit. But the

---

[11] Dt 34:4.
[12] While it is true that all three Persons of the Trinity are involved in revealing divine truth to a prophet, still this activity is appropriated to the Holy Spirit, since the very name inspiration denotes a kind of breathing which is a manner of proceeding appropriate to the Holy Spirit. Moreover, it is appropriate to love that it prompt one to action. And so, since the gift of inspiration is not merely a gift of understanding but a gift prompting the prophet to speak or write, this gift is rightly appropriated to the Holy Spirit. Finally, it is appropriate to a spirit to animate and give life, and the gift of inspiration is a vivification in the knowledge of divine things.
[13] 2 Tm 3:16.
[14] 2 Pt 1:20–21. Cf. Mt 22:43–44; Mk 12:36; Acts 1:16.

mission of the Spirit is ultimately to reveal the Persons from whom He proceeds. And since the Holy Spirit proceeds from the Father and the Son, He is sent in order to reveal the Father through revealing the Son: "But when the Counselor comes, whom I shall send to you from the Father, even the Spirit of truth, who proceeds from the Father, he will bear witness to me."[15] Thus St. Basil the Great writes: "As the Father is seen in the Son, so the Son is seen in the Spirit. . . . As we speak of worship in the Son because the Son is the image of the Father, so we speak of worship in the Spirit because the Spirit is the manifestation of the divinity of the Lord. Through the light of the Spirit we behold the Son, the splendor of God's glory; and through the Son, the very stamp of the Father, we are led to him who is the source."[16]

And so every prophet ultimately acts in order to reveal the Person of the Son, Jesus Christ. And since the Person of the Son has both a divine and human nature, it follows that every prophet acts in order to reveal the incarnate Son of God. It is because of this that the Church teaches that "all Sacred Scripture is but one book, and this one book is Christ, because 'all divine Scripture speaks of Christ, and all divine Scripture is fulfilled in Christ.'"[17]

From all these considerations, it is clear that all prophecy points toward Christ and is fulfilled in Christ. And all the prophets were sent in order to announce the coming of Jesus Christ. Therefore, the greatest of the prophets is the one who most perfectly reveals the Person of the Incarnate Word,

---

[15] Jn 15:26.
[16] *On the Holy Spirit*, ch. 26, n. 64: PG 32, 186.
[17] *CCC* 134 (citing Hugh of St. Victor, *De arca Noe*, 2,8).

Jesus Christ. This helps us to understand and explain why it is that John the Baptist holds a preeminent place among the prophets.

The Greatest among the Prophets

Jesus is not reserved in His praise for John when, according to the text of St. Luke's Gospel, He says: "I tell you, among those born of women no prophet is greater than John; yet he who is least in the kingdom of God is greater than he."[18] This text, based upon the Latin Vulgate and many ancient Greek and Latin texts as well, expressly calls John the greatest of the prophets, while still somehow asserting that John is not among, nor even equal to, those in the Kingdom of God. This helps to explain the text of St. Matthew which simply calls him the greatest among those born of women. Jesus seems to be saying here that among those born of women, John was gifted with the greatest gift of prophecy, but insofar as he was a prophet, and waited for the fulfillment of the kingdom of God from afar, he was, as yet, not a member of the kingdom of God. As St. Paul would put it: "God had foreseen something better for us, that apart from us they should not be made perfect."[19] Nevertheless, among all the prophets, John alone would see and inherit what he previously foresaw. He was simultaneously among those who belonged to the Old Covenant and the New Covenant, which is why Jesus says that John was a kind of boundary:

---

[18] Lk 7:28.
[19] Heb 11:40.

"The law and the prophets were until John."[20] Moreover, Jesus had said to His apostles that "many prophets and kings longed to see what you see, and did not see it, and to hear what you hear, and did not hear it."[21] But John would have this longing fulfilled because he beheld the Christ and heard Him speak. John lived to witness the beginnings of the Messiah's public ministry, which moved him to proclaim: "He must increase, and I must decrease."[22] And so, John was the greatest of the prophets because he both foresaw and saw, desired and received.[23]

It is interesting that although nearly all of the Old Testament prophets wrote down their oracles, St. John did not see the need to do so. We have no book from John as we had from Isaiah and Jeremiah and the other major and minor prophets. This indicates that John knew there would be no need for him to write, since writing is for the sake of communicating for those far off in place or time, but John knew that his words would be fulfilled in the very sight of those to whom he preached. There was no need for future generations to read the preaching of John, since that very generation to whom John spoke would witness its fulfillment. Moreover, while it was typical for great prophets to perform miracles as a witness to the truth of the things he would speak, John performed no miracles, though in some sense his very life

---

[20] Lk 16:16.
[21] Lk 10:24.
[22] Jn 3:30.
[23] When comparing John to Moses, St. Thomas says that "John pertained to the New Testament, whose ministry is preferable even to that of Moses, as one more beholding the unveiled face [of the Lord]" (*ST*, IIa-IIae, q. 174, a. 4, ad. 3).

was miraculous since it seemed to be above the capacity of human virtue. The reason seems to be that his words would be verified in the very sight of the people so that there was no need for miracles to certify what he had foretold: "John did no sign, but everything that John said about this man was true."[24] These facts point to the reality that John was unlike every other prophet. All of them had foretold the coming of Christ from afar, but John foretold it as something near, and almost present. And he himself witnessed and obtained the very blessing which he foresaw and foretold.

Doubting John?

In spite of John's obvious prophetic knowledge of the Christ, some texts have been the occasion for certain men to assert that John had his doubts about who Jesus was. Two texts in particular have been stumbling blocks. The first text is from the first chapter of John, where John the Baptist says: "I did not know him."[25] The second text is reported by both Luke and Matthew and states: "Now when John heard in prison about the deeds of the Christ, he sent word by his disciples and said to him: 'Are you he who is to come, or shall we look for another?'"[26]

What is the meaning of the text: "I did not know him?" What kind of knowledge is John speaking about? The full text reads:

---

[24] Jn 10:41.
[25] Jn 1:33.
[26] Mt 11:2–3; see Lk 7:19–20.

"I myself did not know him; but for this I came baptizing with water, that he might be revealed to Israel." And John bore witness, "I saw the Spirit descend as a dove from heaven, and it remained on him. I myself did not know him; but he who sent me to baptize with water said to me, 'He on whom you see the Spirit descend and remain, this is he who baptizes with the Holy Spirit.' And I have seen and have borne witness that this is the Son of God."[27]

Clearly, John knew the Christ in one sense and did not know him in another. He came baptizing with water to reveal the Christ to Israel, so he knew that the Christ was coming and that he was the Son of God. Not only this, but before he saw the Spirit descend upon Jesus in visible form, he already recognized him as the Christ, for he said to Jesus before the Spirit descended in visible form: "I need to be baptized by you, and do you come to me?"[28] But there were clearly some things John did not know about Jesus.

First of all, because John was baptizing for the repentance of sin, and he knew Jesus was without sin, John at first does not want to baptize Jesus. He whose mission was to prepare the way of the Lord, to make crooked ways straight and the rough places smooth, tries to prevent Jesus from being baptized by him. John himself becomes an obstacle to the way of the Lord! And so John did not yet understand that Jesus came to take the sins of the world upon Himself, to be reckoned among sinners. After this time, however, John

---

[27] Jn 1:31–34.
[28] Mt 3:14.

knows Jesus as the Lamb of God, the fulfillment of the Paschal Lamb who would be sacrificed for sins.[29] Secondly, as the text above states, John did not yet understand that Jesus Himself would baptize with the Holy Spirit until he saw the Spirit descend upon Jesus in visible form. So for these reasons, John claims not to have known Jesus.

The second text is more difficult. Here is the full text as found in Matthew's Gospel:

> Now when John heard in prison about the deeds of the Christ, he sent word by his disciples and said to him, "Are you he who is to come, or shall we look for another?" And Jesus answered them, "Go and tell John what you hear and see: the blind receive their sight and the lame walk, lepers are cleansed and the deaf hear, and the dead are raised up, and the poor have good news preached to them. And blessed is he who takes no offense at me." As they went away, Jesus began to speak to the crowds concerning John: "What did you go out into the wilderness to behold? A reed shaken by the wind? Why then did you go out? To see a man clothed in soft raiment? Behold, those who wear soft raiment are in kings' houses. Why then did you go out? To see a prophet? Yes, I tell you, and more than a prophet. This is he of whom it is written, 'Behold, I send my messenger before thy face, who shall prepare

---

[29] St. Peter seems to have been subject to this same ignorance after it was revealed to him by the Father that Jesus was the Son of God. For, after this revelation, Peter immediately resists Jesus when Jesus begins to speak about His passion and death (see Mt 16:13–23).

thy way before thee.' Truly, I say to you, among those born of women there has risen no one greater than John the Baptist; yet he who is least in the kingdom of heaven is greater than he. From the days of John the Baptist until now the kingdom of heaven has suffered violence, and men of violence take it by force. For all the prophets and the law prophesied until John; and if you are willing to accept it, he is Elijah who is to come. He who has ears to hear, let him hear.[30]

Some read this text as implying that John began to have doubts about Jesus after he was confined to prison. But this interpretation is hardly consistent with the immediate high praise that Jesus gives to John after the messengers leave. Throughout the Gospels, whenever someone lacks faith in Him, Jesus always corrects them. He does not praise them. Moreover, John does not say "shall I look for another" but rather "should we look for another." This shows that he has his disciples in mind when he asks the question. In fact, many fathers and doctors of the Church interpret John's words as an instruction to these two disciples rather than as a question for himself. This comes out even more clearly in St. Luke's Gospel, which places this episode after the raising of the son of the widow of Naim.[31] There it says that some of John's disciples told John about the signs Jesus was performing, including this resurrection miracle. Therefore, John already knew about the many signs Jesus was doing. What then would have been added by the message of Jesus: the

---

[30] Mt 11:2–15.
[31] See Lk 7:11–17.

lame walk, the blind regain their sight, the dead are raised, etc.? There would be no additional information for him in Jesus's message back to John. Therefore, the more reasonable explanation is that John wanted these two disciples to see the signs Jesus was working firsthand so that they would transfer their allegiance to Jesus from him. Recall too that some of John's disciples had been jealous of Jesus for John's sake:

> Now a discussion arose between John's disciples and a Jew over purifying. And they came to John, and said to him, "Rabbi, he who was with you beyond the Jordan, to whom you bore witness, here he is, baptizing, and all are going to him." John answered, "No one can receive anything except what is given him from heaven. You yourselves bear me witness that I said: 'I am not the Christ, but I have been sent before him.' He who has the bride is the bridegroom; the friend of the bridegroom, who stands and hears him, rejoices greatly at the bridegroom's voice; therefore this joy of mine is now full. He must increase, but I must decrease."[32]

This episode is reminiscent of the event recorded in Numbers 11 when Joshua was jealous for Moses's sake because some men were prophesying in the camp, apart from the other elders. Moses responds in a vein similar to John. Far from being jealous of Jesus, John instead tries to convince his disciples to leave him and to follow Jesus. They had become so attached to him that it was hard for them to believe that

---

[32] Jn 3:25–30.

John was not the Christ. Notice also a small detail: Jesus praises John only after the messengers leave. This seems to have been because he knew that such high praise of John would make it harder for them to leave John for Jesus.

That being said, there is something else instructive about John's question to Jesus: "Are you he who is to come, or shall we look for another?" John knew that he was at the boundary of the Old and New Testaments. He knew that during his lifetime he would see the beginnings of the New Covenant but not its full ratification through the Paschal mystery. Therefore, John, knowing he was about to die, wondered whether Jesus would humble Himself so low that He would even descend among the dead in His own person, just as he was surprised that Jesus would humble Himself so low as to sacramentally anticipate His death and descent to the dead through baptism. This is exactly the interpretation Pope St. Gregory would give to John's words: "He asked as one ignorant whether Jesus would be the one who would descend to hell in his own person."[33] Perhaps, thought John, it would be more fitting for someone else (maybe even John himself) to be His messenger among the dead rather than for Jesus to go there in His own person. This also illuminates the text of Luke which places John's question immediately after the resurrection of the son of the widow of Naim. For it was natural for John to wonder whether Jesus would raise him from the dead in the same way as he raised this young man—namely, without himself descending to the dead.

---

[33] *Homilies on the Gospel*, Bk. I, *Hom.* 6 (PL 76, 1095).

More than a Prophet

We have seen that a prophet sees and announces things far from human knowledge yet revealed to him by God. And this is what John does. Yet, he does more than this, as the words of Jesus testify. John is more than a prophet. First of all, John is more than a prophet because he sees, at least in part, the fulfillment of the very things he foresaw and announced. He both foresaw and saw: as someone belonging to both the Old Testament, he foresaw the coming of Christ, but as someone belonging to the New Testament, he saw His coming in the flesh.

But there are other ways in which John is more than a prophet. And Jesus gives an indication of this by what He asserts next: "This is he of whom it is written, 'Behold, I send my messenger before thy face, who shall prepare thy way before thee.'" The Greek word used here and translated as "messenger" is ἄγγελος, the same word which is often translated as "angel." In fact, some early writers actually thought that Jesus was asserting that John was an incarnate angel, not a human being! Setting this interpretation aside, it is worth noting that angels are represented in Scripture as standing above the prophets and priests. For example, it was by angels that the law was revealed to Moses on Mount Sanai, and that God spoke to Abraham on Mount Moriah.[34] By referring to John as an angel, Jesus implies that John stands above the other prophets as one standing more immediately in the presence of God.

---

[34] See Acts 7:53; Gal 3:19.

Finally, John seems to be more than a prophet because he is not only a prophet but also a priest. Indeed, John is the true and last high priest of the Old Covenant, whose glory was to fade, as Jesus increased and John decreased. These matters will be the subject of the following chapters.

Chapter 5

Behold, I Send My Angel

If you pay attention to the way Jesus speaks about others in the Gospels, you begin to notice that while He is very kind and compassionate to sinners, He is also very quick to point out to people that they are sinners. As a result, we do not often read about Jesus praising people for their virtues. This is even more pronounced when we look at the way Jesus evaluates those who follow Him most closely. Nearly every time Jesus evaluates the moral qualities of His apostles, Jesus is very reserved in His praise and rather firm in His criticisms. For example, when St. Peter confesses Jesus to be the Christ, the Son of God, Jesus ascribes Peter's act of faith as a gift from the Father and then shortly thereafter calls Peter Satan. In fact, Jesus tends to reserve His highest praise for those who are outside of the Jewish people. The Gospels tell us that Jesus marveled at the faith of the centurion[1] and that He calls the Canaanite woman's faith great.[2] Perhaps this is because they did more with less. They had so little light from revelation, and yet they produced great acts of faith.

But the most notable exception to Jesus's reserved use of praise is the person of John the Baptist. Never once does

---

[1] See Mt 8:10 and Lk 7:9.
[2] Mt 15:28.

Jesus criticize John, even in circumstances where we might be tempted to criticize him. For example, some early Christian writers claimed that John was having a crisis of faith when from prison he sent two disciples to ask Jesus if He was the one who is to come or should we wait for another. Jesus does not respond as if that is what happened. On the contrary (in a text we have already quoted above), Jesus uses this opportunity to heap the highest praise upon John:

> Now when John heard in prison about the deeds of the Christ, he sent word by his disciples and said to him, "Are you he who is to come, or shall we look for another?" And Jesus answered them, "Go and tell John what you hear and see: the blind receive their sight and the lame walk, lepers are cleansed and the deaf hear, and the dead are raised up, and the poor have good news preached to them. And blessed is he who takes no offense at me." As they went away, Jesus began to speak to the crowds concerning John: "What did you go out into the wilderness to behold? A reed shaken by the wind? Why then did you go out? To see a man clothed in soft raiment? Behold, those who wear soft raiment are in kings' houses. Why then did you go out? To see a prophet? Yes, I tell you, and more than a prophet. This is he of whom it is written, 'Behold, I send my angel before thy face, who shall prepare thy way before thee.' Truly, I say to you, among those born of women there has risen no one greater than John the Baptist; yet he who is least in the kingdom of heaven is greater than he. From the days of John the Baptist

until now the kingdom of heaven has suffered violence, and men of violence take it by force. For all the prophets and the law prophesied until John; and if you are willing to accept it, he is Elijah who is to come. He who has ears to hear, let him hear."[3]

Jesus points out, among other things, that John is so great that he is the subject of prophecy. In particular, the prophecy which Jesus points to as identifying John is the text of Malachi 3:1: "Behold, I send my angel before my face."[4] The word *angel* simply means messenger, but the typical understanding of this text in Jesus's time seemed to refer this prophecy to a superhuman creature belonging to the hosts of heaven. This current of interpretation was so strong that even early Christian commentators such as Origen took it to mean that John was actually an incarnate angel![5] And while this reading cannot stand (for the prologue of John says that John was "a *man* sent by God"), it does contain truth insofar as John's life was so absorbed in heavenly realities that he deserved to be ranked alongside the angels of heaven.

So exactly what is Jesus asserting about John when he says that he is the fulfillment of the prophecy of Malachi? Let us examine the context of this prophecy.

> Behold, I send my angel to prepare the way before me,
> and the Lord whom you seek will suddenly come to

---

[3] Mt 11:2–15.
[4] Cf. Mt 11:10; Mk 1:2; Lk 7:27.
[5] There are a few defenders of this thesis even today. Suffice it to say, the Scriptures clearly reveal the entirely human origins of John, including his need to be sanctified in his mother's womb.

his temple; the angel of the covenant in whom you delight, behold, he is coming, says the Lord of hosts. But who can endure the day of his coming, and who can stand when he appears? For he is like a refiner's fire and like fullers' lye he will sit as a refiner and purifier of silver, and he will purify the sons of Levi and refine them like gold and silver, till they present right offerings to the Lord. Then the offering of Judah and Jerusalem will be pleasing to the Lord as in the days of old and as in former years.[6]

The first thing the prophet says about this angel is that he is sent from God. Interestingly, the first person one might think this prophecy refers to is actually the angel Gabriel. It was the angel Gabriel who "was sent from God"[7] to the Virgin Mary to prepare the way for the coming of the Lord. And once Mary gave her fiat, suddenly the Lord entered into her womb and made her into His most perfect temple. And yet, Jesus says that this prophecy refers to John the Baptist. Nevertheless, there is a clear likeness between the mission of the angel Gabriel and the mission of St. John. Both are sent to prepare the way for the coming of the Lord to His temple. This implies a certain spiritual affinity between St. John and the angel Gabriel.

The prophecy goes on to speak about the "angel of the covenant." Is this the same angel as at the beginning of the prophecy, or does it refer to the Lord who comes to His temple? Perhaps it can refer to both, but since the only angel

---

[6] Mal 3:1–5.
[7] Lk 1:26.

referred to so far is the angel who is sent to prepare the way of the Lord, it makes sense to continue reading this as referring to St. John. He is called the "angel of the covenant." Throughout Scripture, we read about several covenants into which the Lord entered. He entered into a covenant with Noah and with the living things after the flood; He entered into a covenant with Abraham and renewed it with Isaac and Jacob; He entered into a covenant with the whole people through Moses. The Lord entered into a covenant with King David, assuring an everlasting kingdom through his descendants. King Jehoiada made a covenant with the Lord and the people, as did Ezra. The prophets Baruch and Ezekiel speak about an eternal covenant which seems to be a kind of renewal of a prior covenant. The prophets Isaiah and Jeremiah speak about a new covenant which shall be eternal and far superior to the prior covenant so as to supersede it, as St. Paul points out in the epistle to the Hebrews. So to which covenant is the prophet Malachi referring when he speaks of the angel of the covenant?

If we look in the preceding chapter, we find that the covenant to which Malachi is referring is a covenant made with Levi, the priestly tribe of Israel:

> Then you will know that I sent you this commandment because I have a covenant with Levi, says the Lord of hosts. My covenant with him was one of life and peace; fear I put in him, and he feared me, and stood in awe of my name. True doctrine was in his mouth, and no dishonesty was found upon his lips. He walked with me in integrity and in uprightness,

and turned many away from evil. For the lips of the priest are to keep knowledge, and instruction is to be sought from his mouth, because he is the angel of the Lord of hosts. But you have turned aside from the way, and have caused many to falter by your instruction. You have made void the covenant of Levi, says the Lord of hosts.[8]

This covenant was established by the Lord as we read in Numbers 3:12–13: "It is I who have chosen the Levites from the Israelites in place of every first-born that opens the womb among the Israelites. The Levites, therefore, are mine, because every first-born is mine. When I slew all the first-born in the land of Egypt, I made all the first-born in Israel sacred to me, both of man and of beast. They belong to me; I am the Lord."[9] As Malachi describes it, this covenant is a covenant with the priests that they (and the people) might find "life and peace." On their side, the priests were to revere the Lord, and to teach "true doctrine," and to walk in "integrity and uprightness." Moreover, he specifically calls the priest an "angel" of the Lord. Thus, the "angel of the covenant" is a priest who shall fulfill or reestablish the priestly covenant made with Levi.

---

[8] Mal 2:4–8.
[9] Cf. Nm 8:17–19. There is some evidence that the Levites were specially dedicated to the Lord as a result of their purging of the people from the sin of worshipping the golden calf (see Ex 32). But the Lord seems to indicate that the covenant with Levi was founded upon the Passover, since the Levites are considered by the Lord as the "first-born" of Israel who have been redeemed through the blood of the Passover lamb.

Malachi continues, saying that this angel of the covenant is one "in whom you delight." For as the angel Gabriel foretold, "many will rejoice in his birth," and as Jesus said, John "was a burning and shining lamp, and for a while you were content to rejoice in his light."[10] Even Herod, as wicked as he was, "was very much perplexed, yet he liked to listen to him."[11] So John produced delight in others by the purity of his life and the clarity and force of his teaching.

"But who can endure the day of his coming, and who can stand when he appears? For he is like a refiner's fire and like fullers' lye." After describing John as one who comes to restore the holy priesthood and covenant, Malachi continues to describe how this will be done: by purifying the people and the priests. This prompts a question about who can endure such a purification, for the demands of the life to which John was calling the people were great. Therefore, he is compared to a "refiner's fire" or a "fuller's lye," powerful agents which totally destroy impurities. For those who were wholly given over to this impure way of life, the ministry of John was fatal: "Even now the axe is laid to the root of the trees; every tree therefore that does not bear good fruit is cut down and thrown into the fire."[12] But for those who were weak, but retained their love for God and their desire to serve him, John was "a refiner and purifier of silver, and he will purify the sons of Levi and refine them like gold and silver." Thus, he would remove what was an impediment to the divine life and confirm what was good and pleasing to

---

[10] Jn 5:35.
[11] Mk 6:20.
[12] Mt 3:10.

God within them. Notice that the prophet Malachi refers to both silver and gold. Perhaps the silver refers to the common priesthood which would belong to all the baptized: "You are a chosen race, a royal priesthood, a holy nation."[13] On the other hand, the gold may refer to the ministerial priesthood belonging to the ordained: "Do not neglect the gift you have, which was given you by prophetic utterance when the council of elders laid their hands upon you."[14] And so John's preaching and baptizing was for the sake of purifying the people, but especially the Levitical priests. We have some indication that John was successful in his endeavors from the Acts of the Apostles, which mentions that "a large group of priests were becoming obedient to the faith."[15] Jesus also seemed to have a special desire for the conversion of the priests. For example, when He healed a leper, Jesus tells him: "Go show yourself to the priest, and offer the gift that Moses prescribed; that will be proof for them."[16]

This purifying action would continue until "they present right offerings to the Lord. Then the offering of Judah and Jerusalem will be pleasing to the Lord as in the days of old and as in former years." The ultimate goal of this purification is that the priests may offer an acceptable and pleasing sacrifice to God. The offering of an acceptable and pleasing sacrifice is an act of the virtue of religion, which establishes a right order between man and God. And this pleasing sacrifice would find its completion not in the work of John but

---

[13] 1 Pt 2:9.
[14] 1 Tm 4:14.
[15] Acts 6:7.
[16] Mt 8:4; cf. Mk 1:44 and Lk 5:14.

in the sacrifice of Christ on the cross and in the Mass, both of which would take place in Judah, and more specifically in Jerusalem. What does the expression "as in the days of old and as in former years" refer to? Perhaps to the time when the Levitical priesthood was first established under Aaron. Or perhaps it refers to a prior time when Adam and Eve still lived in innocence and walked with God. For the sacrifice of Christ perfectly restores us to God's friendship.

It is interesting to note that Malachi describes the purification of the people in terms of the purification of precious metals such as gold and silver. I once heard a story told by a silversmith that the way he can tell that the purification is complete is that he can see his image reflected in the molten silver or gold. So too, God's purification of our souls is complete when He can finally see His image in our souls.

Priests and Angels

In the text of the prophet Malachi cited above, he refers to the priest as an "angel." Taking up the language of the prophet Malachi, Dionysius the Areopagite (more commonly known now as Pseudo-Dionysius) asserts that just as the angelic hierarchies receive divine light and revelation from above and pass these on to lower ranks of creatures, so too the sacred hierarchies of bishop, priest, and deacon receive divine revelation and light and pass these on to those subject to them. Therefore, the ecclesiastical hierarchy is an extension of the celestial hierarchy into the realm of sensible and mortal creatures: "The Divinity made the heavenly hierarchies known to us, and made our own hierarchy a ministerial colleague of these divine hierarchies by an assimilation, to the extent that is humanly feasible, to their godlike priesthood."[17] Thus, just as priests can be called angels, since they are messengers of the most high, so angels can be called priests, since they mediate divine gifts to men. This same teaching was developed and confirmed in the writings of later doctors of the Church, most notably, St. Thomas Aquinas: "The highest order of our hierarchy has something similar to the lowest order of the heavenly hierarchy, and therefore, a priest is called an angel."[18] "A priest, inasmuch as he is a mediator between God and the people, has the name 'angel.'"[19]

According to this teaching, every hierarchy is distinguished into three. Thus, there is a highest rank of angels, a middle rank of angels, and a lowest rank of angels. To the lowest rank belongs the activity of purifying or preparing the matter. To the middle rank, the office of illuminating or instructing. And to the highest rank belongs the activity of perfecting. Thus, also, it belongs to the deacons to purify by removing error and impurity of life. It belongs to the priests to illuminate by instructing in the sacred mysteries and administering the sacraments. And it belongs to the bishop, as high priest, to perfect by leading the souls under his care to a perfect union with God by the excellence of his preaching, revealing the sacred mysteries of the Scriptures, and super-eminent holiness of life: "In the ecclesiastical hierarchy orders are distinguished according to whether

---

[17] Pseudo-Dionysius, *The Celestial Hierarchy*, ch. 1.
[18] *In II Sent.*, d. 9, q. 1, a. 3, c.
[19] *ST*, IIIa, q. 22, a. 1, ad. 1.

one purifies, illumines or perfects. For the order of deacon is purifying, the order of priest is illuminative, and the order of bishop is perfective."[20]

Of course, the highest order contains the full power of those beneath it, so that all three activities of purifying, illuminating, and perfecting are in the power of the highest priest. It is just these activities which are attributed to John the Baptist. Concerning his action of purifying, we read: "he will sit as a refiner and purifier of silver, and he will purify the sons of Levi and refine them like gold and silver."[21] Moreover, by his baptism for the remission of sins, we find him cleansing the hearts of the people. Concerning his act of illuminating, we read: "with many other exhortations, he preached good news to the people."[22] And about his perfecting activity, the angel Gabriel says that John will "make ready for the Lord a people prepared,"[23] that is, perfected.

Of course, John does all of this in anticipation of Christ, and as yet a member of the old covenant, he cannot bring about the full perfection which only Christ will later bring. For John exhorted the people by saying: "He that has two coats let him give it to him that has none; and he that has food, let him do the same,"[24] but Jesus would later instruct His disciples that if an adversary "takes your coat, give him your cloak as well."[25] And to the tax collectors, John said:

---

[20] *ST*, Ia, q. 108, a. 2.
[21] Mal 3:3.
[22] Lk 3:18.
[23] Lk 1:17.
[24] Lk 3:11.
[25] Mt 5:40.

"Collect no more than is appointed you,"[26] but Jesus caused the tax collector Zacchaeus to give half his belongings to the poor and pay back fourfold any he had defrauded. To the soldiers, John said: "Rob no one by violence or by false accusation, and be content with your wages,"[27] but Jesus prompted a centurion to make an act of humility and faith greater than any in Israel. For the power of Christ was such as to impart to the inward heart of man the strength to do that which nature finds repugnant. Therefore, John is like the doctor's assistant who prepares the patient, while the divine physician comes to heal completely. In this, it is made clear that the mission of John is a preparation for but not a beginning of the new covenant of grace: "The least in the kingdom of God is greater than John."[28] Yet to the crowds, even though the injunctions of John were not so great as those which Jesus would later give, still they seemed wonderful and divine to those who had not yet experienced divine grace.

Nevertheless, John really does act as the pinnacle of the old covenant, for the Law and the prophets were up until John, as if John were their ultimate terminus. As such, he performs the acts appropriate to the high priest, the most perfect action which the priesthood of the old covenant would allow. For while the priesthood in Jerusalem had become corrupt, God appointed one as a high priest in the desert. It is John as high priest which we shall consider in the next chapter.

---

[26] Lk 3:13.
[27] Lk 3:14.
[28] Mt 11:11.

Chapter 6

John the High Priest

Many Fathers of the Church (including Ambrose, Augustine, Chrysostom, and Bede) assert that Zechariah, the father of John the Baptist, was designated as high priest through what is written in the opening chapter of the Gospel of St. Luke. It follows that his only son, John, would be the rightful inheritor of the title of high priest. In this chapter, I intend to defend that claim and also to explain the significance of this truth for understanding the person and mission of John the Baptist. But first, it will be helpful to trace the history of the priesthood, beginning with Aaron and continuing until the time of John.

What Is a Priest?

A priest is a mediator between God and man who unites man to God by means of sacrifice. In the book of Deuteronomy, Moses says: "I was the mediator and stood between the Lord and you at that time to show you his words,"[1] and in the epistle to the Hebrews, it is written: "For every high priest taken from among men, is ordained for men in the things that appertain to God, that he might offer up gifts

---
[1] Dt 5:5.

and sacrifices for sins."² St. Thomas says simply that a priest is a mediator between God and the people.³ The role of the priest as mediator was to exchange gifts between men and God. From men, he offered up to God sacrifices—for example, a young, unblemished bull. From God, he handed down to men divine teaching and blessings. The sacrifices offered to God were intended to acknowledge that every human possession comes from God, so that in justice we owe all that we have and are to God. The gifts of divine revelation and grace are intended to give men an understanding of who God is and to give us the means to live in a way pleasing to Him. This exchange, therefore, places us in right relation to God so that we are able to live in communion with Him. The mission of St. John is reminiscent of this goal of the priesthood: "to turn the hearts of fathers toward children and the disobedient to the understanding of the righteous, to prepare a people fit for the Lord."⁴

A Brief History of the Priesthood in Scripture

The first mention of a sacrifice being offered in Scripture is the offerings of Cain and Abel in the fourth chapter of Genesis. There, although Cain was the firstborn (to whom the role of priest was usually assigned),⁵ nevertheless, it was Abel's sacrifice which was pleasing to God, while Cain's was not. After this, the next mention of sacrifice was that of Noah (a firstborn) after the great flood. Then there is

---

[2] Heb 5:1.
[3] *ST*, q. 102, a. 4.
[4] Lk 1:17.
[5] See Nm 3:12.

the mention of Melchizedek who offered gifts of bread and wine. Melchizedek was the first person to be called a priest in Scripture. Some ancient Jewish sources speculate that he was none other than the firstborn son of Noah, Shem, who (according to the biblical chronology) would have been an old man at the time Abraham meets Melchizedek. Then we read of offerings made by Abraham, Isaac, and Jacob (all firstborn sons). The next mention of priesthood and of sacrifice is found in the book of Exodus, in which Moses, and after him, Aaron, are authorized by God to offer sacrifice. Moses was the younger brother of Aaron, and yet he was clearly a priest. Once again, the priesthood of the firstborn seems not to have been an absolute rule. Moses was the first to establish, at God's command, a formal priesthood associated with the covenant of the Lord through the line of Aaron. This line of priests is distinguished from the order according to Melchizedek mentioned in Psalm 110 and in the Epistle to the Hebrews.

Beginning with Aaron, God commands that he and his sons shall serve Him as priests and that if anyone offers sacrifice other than a male descendant of Aaron, he shall be destroyed. This is the theme of Numbers 16, in which Korah and the other Levites claim the right to the priesthood and are killed by the Lord. This forceful episode concludes with this warning: "No one who is not a priest, who is not of the descendants of Aaron, should draw near to burn incense before the Lord, lest he become as Korah and as his company."[6] In the book of Numbers, chapter 35, for

---

[6] Nm 16:40.

the first time, the title high priest is used. It clearly refers first to Aaron but also implies that from among the sons of Aaron, one was to be chosen as the high priest. Eleazar is the one who succeeds his father Aaron as high priest, followed by his son Phinehas. At this point, due to the zealous act of Phinehas, God designates Phinehas and his descendants as the bearers of the high priesthood evermore: "Phinehas the son of Eleazar, son of Aaron the priest, has turned back my wrath from the people of Israel, in that he was jealous with my jealousy among them, so that I did not consume the people of Israel in my jealousy. Therefore say, 'Behold, I give to him my covenant of peace; and it shall be to him, and to his descendants after him, the covenant of a perpetual priesthood, because he was jealous for his God, and made atonement for the people of Israel.'"[7]

Commenting upon this designation, the book of Sirach makes it clear that it is the high priesthood that shall belong to the descendants of Phinehas: "Therefore a covenant of peace was established with him, that he should be leader of the sanctuary and of his people, that he and his descendants should have the dignity of the priesthood for ever."[8]

At the time of Samuel, however, the high priest was Eli, who seems to have been a descendant of Itamar, Eleazar's brother and Phinehas's uncle.[9] How or why this transfer took place is unclear. But there are indications that God is

---

[7] Nm 25:11–13.
[8] Sir 45:24.
[9] This can be inferred from the indication that Ahimelech was both a descendant of Ithamar (see 1 Chr 24:3) and a descendant of Eli (see 1 Sm 14:3 and 22:20).

not pleased with this line.[10] God punishes both Eli and his sons with death for their moral corruption so that the grandson of Eli, Ahitub, inherits the office of high priest. This line continues until the Temple of Solomon, at which point Abiathar (still a descendant of Eli) is removed for conspiring against King Solomon and is replaced with Zadok, a descendant of both Eleazar and Phinehas.

Between Zadok and the Babylonian exile, it seems that the high priest remained a descendant of Phinehas. During the Babylonian exile, it is not clear whether or not someone was designated as "titular" high priest. Obviously, there was no worship in the Temple at this time (since it had been destroyed), so the next clear indication we have of a high priest is Joshua, son of Jehozadak, once the second Temple had been built. Joshua was clearly approved by the Lord,[11] who expressly calls him the "High Priest." Nevertheless, as time went on, those recognized as high priest, whether good or bad, often were appointed by political rulers, even gentiles, rather than by the decree of the Lord.[12] It seems that the office of high priest became more and more political and about exercising temporal power. So much was this the case that Jesus, when He is about to appoint His apostles as leaders of the Church who would replace the Jewish leaders, warns them about exercising authority as the Gentiles do.[13]

---

[10] See 1 Sm 2:22–36.
[11] See Hg 2:4 and Zec 6:11.
[12] See, for example, 1 Mc 10:18–20, where the high priest Jonathan was appointed by Alexander.
[13] See Lk 22:25–30.

John as High Priest

This brief history shows that by the time John was born, the office of high priest had departed very far from the intention which God had for this office. And perhaps those who were holding the office at the time of John's birth were even illegitimate usurpers rather than being true high priests in the eyes of the Lord. This brings us to the Gospel of St. Luke, which clearly teaches that John begins to assume the office of the high priest, albeit outside of the Temple.

It is significant that St. Luke mentions that there were two high priests at this time: Annas and Caiphas. Now it was not permitted under the law that there be two high priests at the same time, and therefore the words of St. Luke should not be understood to indicate that Annas and Caiphas were acting as high priest simultaneously. But perhaps they were taking turns as high priest, or perhaps they each held that post for a single year but are the two mentioned as being most instrumental in the passion of Jesus. It is better, however, to say that the words of St. Luke indicate that, although they formally held the post of high priest at different times, they were sharing the power of the high priesthood together. And this seems to be shown in the Gospel of John, since Jesus is taken to the house of Annas when He was first arrested, and both were responsible for the condemnation of Jesus. And in this manner, they attempted to circumvent the law.

In the Old Law, as originally promulgated, there was no provision for alternating or yearly high priests. Rather, there was to be a single high priest who ruled until death (see Lv 21:10 and Nm 35:25). And so, by remarking that there were two high priests, St. Luke indicates that neither was acting in accordance with the law and also that they were duplicitous, since the number two signifies deceit. Moreover, this indicates the division of the priesthood which came to be under the Old Law, while in the New Law, there is one, eternal, High Priest and, therefore, only one Church: according to St. Ambrose in his commentary on Luke, "Then, indeed, there were changes in the priesthood, now it is unchangeable." And so, the word of God does not come through the high priests but rather through John, the rightful heir of the high priesthood: "During the high priesthood of Annas and Caiaphas, the word of God came to John the son of Zechariah in the desert."[14] Nevertheless, in spite of their unlawful behavior, God continued to use Caiphas as His unwitting instrument, as St. John remarks: "He did not say this on his own, but since he was High Priest for that year, he prophesied that Jesus was going to die for the nation."[15]

According to many Fathers of the Church, Zechariah is shown by St. Luke to be the true high priest at this time. The first piece of evidence that Zechariah is the true high priest is that Zechariah is identified as a descendant of Aaron belonging to the division of Abijah.[16] This was one of the descendants of Eleazar, and likely of Phinehas as well. The second piece of evidence that Zechariah was the true high priest is the fact that, like Aaron, the first high priest, Zechariah was married to a woman named Elizabeth who was

---
[14] Lk 3:3.
[15] Jn 11:51.
[16] Interestingly, the division immediately after Abijah was the division of Jeshua, or Jesus.

connected to the tribe of Judah.[17] The third piece of evidence that Zechariah was the true high priest is that he was performing the duty proper to the high priest when he went in to offer incense. Many Church Fathers and other ancient sources asserted that Zechariah was performing the office of the high priest when he went in to offer incense.[18] For example, St. Ambrose says: "Zechariah seems here to be designated High Priest, because only the High Priest went into the second tabernacle once every year."[19]

This assertion is significant since it not only implies that God recognized Zechariah as the legitimate heir to Aaron, Eleazar, and Phinehas[20] but also that John, his son, was in fact the one who by right should inherit the office of high priest. The place where Zechariah offers the incense is the second tabernacle where the altar of incense was placed right before the veil of the Ark of the Covenant. And Zechariah is there out of obedience to fulfill his priestly office. St. Luke says that "it happened" that Zechariah was chosen so that "he should offer incense when he went into the temple of the Lord" as if by chance, since this took place by casting lots.

---

[17] See Ex 6:23; 1 Chr 2:10.
[18] They include Origen, Chrysostom, Augustine, Ambrose, Theodoret, Dionysius the Areopagite, Venerable Bede, and Theophylact, as well as the *Protoevangelium of James*.
[19] This opinion of St. Ambrose was also shared by St. Thomas Aquinas, who asserts that Zechariah was exercising the office of high priest.
[20] Josephus reports that the recognized high priest at that time was Joazarum (*Antiquities*, Bk. 17, ch. 8). It may be, however, that he was a usurper, or descended from a usurper, so that in the eyes of God, it was Zechariah who was the true high priest. For at this time, new people were occupying the office of high priest every year (see Jn 11:49 and 18:13).

And although it was by lot that Zechariah was chosen, this was accomplished according to the divine providence which disposes even chance events according to His will. Moreover, by this it is shown that Zechariah did not take this honor upon himself but was chosen by God: "No one takes this honor upon himself but only when called by God."[21]

The altar of incense where Zechariah was making his offering was not located within the veil where the Ark of the Covenant resided, so it was not, strictly speaking, within the Holy of Holies. Nevertheless, there was a special atonement offering made at that altar once per year[22] so that the altar of incense was considered by God as part of the Holy of Holies, as the words of Exodus 30:10 imply: "It shall be most holy to the Lord." This was also the opinion of St. John Chrysostom: "This man Zechariah came into the Holy of Holies."[23] Moreover, the fact that Zechariah offered incense at the altar of incense does not rule out the possibility that he previously also entered into the Holy of Holies.

One fascinating detail in St. Luke's account is that the multitude became anxious at his delay. This is a bit of circumstantial evidence that Zechariah was also in the Holy of Holies. For when the high priest would offer incense in the Holy of Holies on the Day of Atonement, it was stipulated that his prayer would be brief. This was because if the high priest were to die while inside of the Holy of Holies, it would be the duty of the other priests to bring his body

---

[21] Heb 5:4.
[22] Some ancient sources claim that this took place on the Day of Atonement.
[23] *On the Incomprehensible Nature of God*, II.9.

out without entering into the Holy of Holies (they had a rope tied to his ankle for this very purpose). So the high priest had to make a brief prayer lest the people and other priests wonder whether he was still alive. Two ancient Jewish texts speak about this: "He did not make the prayer long so as to frighten Israel."[24] Also, the Jerusalem Talmud states: "Once a certain high priest made a long prayer and [his fellow priests] decided to go in after him—they say this high priest was Shim'on the Righteous. They said to him: 'Why did you pray so long?' He said to them: 'I was praying that the temple of your God would not be destroyed.' They said to him: 'Even so, you should not have prayed so long.'"[25]

So the fact that Luke bothers to include that detail about the wonderment of the people that Zechariah had taken so long is indirect confirmation that he was also in the Holy of Holies that day.

Additional Evidence that John Was the True High Priest

It is often taken for granted that the angel's injunction that John "shall drink no wine nor strong drink"[26] pointed to the fact that John would be a Nazarite. But the requirements for a Nazarite also included eating nothing unclean and never having his hair shaved. And the angel says nothing about these requirements for John. On the other hand, it was a requirement that the high priest abstain from wine and

---

[24] Mishnah, *Yoma* 5.1.
[25] Jerusalem Talmud, *Yoma* 42c.
[26] Lk 1:15.

strong drink: "And the Lord spoke unto Aaron, saying, do not drink wine nor strong drink, thou, nor your sons with you, when you go into the tabernacle of the congregation, lest you die: it shall be a statute forever throughout your generations."[27] If John were to exercise the office of high priest even outside the Temple, it would make sense that he would always have to abstain from wine and strong drink.

Moreover, when God instituted the new Levitical priesthood, the transition was marked by a kind of ritual washing: "And you shall bring Aaron and his sons unto the door of the tabernacle of the congregation, and wash them with water. And you shall put upon Aaron the holy garments, and anoint him, and sanctify him; that he may minister unto me in the priest's office."[28] So it is only fitting that at the transition of priesthoods, the former high priest would ritually wash the new high priest (just as Moses once had washed Aaron). In this case, then, the baptism of Jesus marks a transition of priesthoods.

The Baptism of Jesus and the Ritual of the Scapegoat

However, the clearest evidence that shows us that St. Luke reveals that John was the true high priest comes from the account of the baptism and temptations of Jesus found in the third and fourth chapters of St. Luke's Gospel. St. Luke records that John was preaching a baptism of repentance for

---

[27] Lv 10:8–9.
[28] Ex 40:12, 13.

the forgiveness of sin. He then goes on to describe the baptism of Jesus and the things which immediately followed:

> Now when all the people were baptized, and when Jesus also had been baptized and was praying, the heaven was opened, and the Holy Spirit descended upon him in bodily form, as a dove, and a voice came from heaven, "Thou art my beloved Son; with thee I am well pleased." Jesus, when he began his ministry, was about thirty years of age, being the son (as was supposed) of Joseph, the son of Heli. . . . And Jesus, full of the Holy Spirit, returned from the Jordan, and was led by the Spirit for forty days in the wilderness, [and was] tempted by the devil.[29]

At first glance, this text seems to say nothing about the priesthood of John, but the details of Jesus's baptism make it clear that St. Luke is identifying John with the high priest. The first detail is that Jesus is said to be about thirty years old, and this statement is immediately followed by his lineage. This might seem to be an odd coincidence to a modern reader, but to a first-century Levite in Palestine, it very clearly indicates that Jesus is beginning His ministry as a priest. For a Levite was to assume his duties of ministering before the Lord at the age of thirty (see Nm 4:3), at which time he would present his lineage to verify that he was one of those qualified (see Nm 3:10). Naturally, it would be the office of the high priest to make the ultimate determination if someone had the correct lineage to serve as a priest.

---

[29] Lk 3:21–23; 4:1–2.

After giving the lineage of Jesus, the fourth chapter of St. Luke's Gospel goes on to describe how after John's baptism, Jesus was led into the desert east of Jerusalem, tempted by the devil and, after preaching to the people from the prophet Isaiah, led to the brow of a cliff to be pushed over, only to escape their power. All of these events bear a striking resemblance to the description of the Day of Atonement ritual found in Leviticus 16. According to the ritual, a goat, known as the "scapegoat," was brought before the high priest, who placed his hands on the head of the goat and confessed the sins of the people over it, thereby transferring their sins to the goat. From there, the goat was led into the wilderness, toward the east of the tabernacle: "Let [the high priest] offer the living goat, and putting both hands upon his head, let him confess all the iniquities of the children of Israel, and all their offenses and sins. And praying that they may light on his head, he shall turn him out by a man ready for it. And when the goat has carried all their iniquities into an uninhabited land . . . it shall be let go into the desert."[30]

The goat was destined for Azazel: "the goat on which the lot fell for Azazel shall be presented alive before the Lord to make atonement over it, so that it may be sent away into the wilderness to Azazel."[31] According to Jewish tradition, Azazel was one of the fallen angels. In the book of Enoch, for example, we find this assertion: "The whole earth has been corrupted through the works that were taught by Azazel: to him ascribe all sin."[32] Finally, ancient sources reveal that, in

---

[30] Lv 16:21–22.
[31] Lv 16:10.
[32] Enoch 10:8.

order to prevent the goat from returning to the camp, it was pushed off a cliff.[33] Moreover, the Day of Atonement is the only day of the Jewish calendar for which mortification is commanded, typically in the form of fasting.[34]

Each of the elements of the baptism and temptation of Jesus in the wilderness corresponds exactly to this ritual:

1. John baptizes Jesus, who was sinless, with a baptism of repentance for sin. In this way, Jesus allows Himself to be reckoned among sinners. So also, the scapegoat, which was sinless, has the sins of the people placed upon it by the high priest.
2. Jesus is led out into the wilderness by the Spirit toward the east of the Temple to be exposed to the temptation of the devil. The scapegoat is led by a man to the east of the tabernacle into the wilderness for the devil Azazel.
3. Jesus fasts for forty days. Fasting is proscribed for the Day of Atonement.
4. After his return, Jesus reads the text of the prophet Isaiah which proclaims liberty and freedom for those who are bound. On the Day of Atonement, the jubilee (the fiftieth year) is announced in which liberty is proclaimed to captives and those bound by debts are freed.[35]

---

[33] For example, see the Mishna (*Yoma* 6:6), Philo in *De Plantatione* 61, and an ancient Jewish source entitled *The Apocalypse of Abraham*.

[34] Lv 23:27–28. From an ancient custom, forty days of fasting was stipulated.

[35] Lv 25:9–10. It is also noteworthy that in the synagogue liturgy, the prophet Isaiah is read about the same time as the Day of Atonement.

5. Jesus is led to the brow of a hill to be thrown down headlong. So also, the scapegoat is lead to a cliff to be thrown down.

All of these elements make it clear that St. Luke saw in the events of Jesus's baptism and temptation a fulfillment of the Day of Atonement ritual. And in this ritual, it is clear that John fulfills the office of the high priest.[36]

In summary, the main evidence that John is the true high priest comes from 1) the fact that his father Zechariah performs the functions of the high priest, and hence John is the one who inherits the office of high priest from his father; and 2) John is shown fulfilling the office of the high priest in the fulfillment of the Day of Atonement ritual.

The Significance of John Being the High Priest

John is in some way the pinnacle of the entire Old Covenant. Jesus Himself testifies that John was a kind of boundary: "The Law and the prophets were until John."[37] He is the greatest and best of the Old Covenant: the greatest prophet, the greatest priest. He was like an angel in human form. As such, he is the perfect representative of all that was best in the Old Covenant. Therefore, the person of John is a privileged locus to whom we should look in order to see God's plan for instituting the Old Covenant and the old priesthood.

---

[36] It is worth noting that other elements of the Day of Atonement ritual reveal a likeness to the crucifixion of Jesus, the other time when Jesus confronts the devil.
[37] Lk 16:16; Mt 11:13.

One important consequence of John being the true high priest is that John exercises his office outside of the Temple. This means that the office of the high priest is separated from the physical Temple in Jerusalem. The earthly Temple had never been intended as God's permanent dwelling. Instead, it served its purpose for a time as a kind of sacrament of the heavenly Temple. God expressly makes the continued existence of the physical Temple conditional upon the fidelity of the people.[38] Yet, while the continued existence of the physical Temple is conditional, the continued existence of the priesthood is not. When the people are unfaithful, God sends John as high priest outside of the Temple to usher in the reign of the true and eternal high priest. This separation of the office of the high priest from the Temple makes possible a universal exercise of the priesthood beyond the physical boundaries of Jerusalem or Judah. Jesus indicates this in His discourse with the Samaritan woman at the well:

> The woman said to him, "Sir, I perceive that you are a prophet. Our fathers worshiped on this mountain; and you say that in Jerusalem is the place where men ought to worship." Jesus said to her, "Woman, believe me, the hour is coming when neither on this mountain nor

---

[38] See, for example, 2 Chr 7:19–21: "But if you turn away and forsake my statutes and commands which I placed before you, if you proceed to venerate and worship strange gods, then I will uproot the people from the land I gave them; I will cast from my sight this house which I have consecrated to my honor, and I will make it a proverb and a byword among all peoples. This temple which is so exalted—everyone passing by it will be amazed and ask: 'Why has the Lord done this to this land and to this house?'"

in Jerusalem will you worship the Father. You worship what you do not know; we worship what we know, for salvation is from the Jews. But the hour is coming, and now is, when the true worshipers will worship the Father in spirit and truth, for such the Father seeks to worship him. God is Spirit, and those who worship him must worship in spirit and truth."[39]

The fact that John is the true high priest also allows St. Luke to make a fruitful comparison between the old and new priesthoods.[40] If someone wants to compare two things, one of the best ways to do this is to compare them in their best or perfect condition. For example, it is better to compare a full-grown orange tree to a full-grown lemon tree (rather than comparing their seeds) if you want to identify significant differences between them. Similarly, if you want to compare the married vocation to a religious vocation, it is best to compare them in their best conditions. It will do very little good to compare a bad marriage to a good religious vocation, or a failed religious vocation to a good marriage. It makes perfect sense then if St. Luke wants to compare the old priesthood to the new priesthood that he should take their perfect representatives: John, the perfection of the old priesthood, and Jesus, the perfection of the new priesthood.

At every stage of their lives—conception, birth, circumcision, and public ministry—St. Luke reveals something

---

[39] Jn 4:19–24.
[40] While well-known to the Fathers of the Church, it is little appreciated today that St. Luke's Gospel focuses especially upon the priesthood of Jesus. One sign of this is that Luke's Gospel begins and ends in the Temple and is often centered around the Temple.

insightful about the differences between the priesthood of John and the priesthood of Jesus. The difference in the way that John and Jesus are conceived reveals that the new priesthood has in itself what the old priesthood had only in figure—namely, the very principle of grace, whereby man is restored to God's favor. For John's father is Zechariah and John prepares the way so that the hearts of fathers and sons may be turned toward one another. But Jesus calls God His Father. In fact, His whole being is to be from and toward His Father. Again, Elizabeth "was barren," while Mary was "full of grace," and while John was conceived carnally by one subject to sin, Jesus was conceived by "the power of the Holy Spirit," in whom is all grace.

The account of Mary's visit to Elizabeth shows the superiority of the new priesthood to the old priesthood with respect to its sanctity, since it is the new priesthood which blesses and sanctifies the old. Thus, the book of Hebrews states: "That which is less is blessed by the superior."[41]

The neighbors who are called to rejoice with Joseph and Mary at the birth of Christ are not kinsfolk but poor shepherds not related to Jesus. On the contrary, those who rejoiced over the birth of John were his kinsfolk and neighbors. The birth of John, rendered wonderful by the old age of his mother, drew the attention of the neighbors and kinsfolk of Elizabeth, for they came together to glorify God's mercy towards her. But the birth of Jesus, having been announced by angels and foretold by a star, drew not only those who were near but also those who were far off—namely, the

---

[41] Heb 7:7.

shepherds and the wise men of the Gentiles. And this signifies the greater universality which the new priesthood enjoys over the old. For the old priesthood ministered only to those of the house of Israel, who were united by bonds of blood, while the new priesthood ministers to all men.

At the beginning of His public ministry, Jesus calls Himself the bridegroom, while John is the "friend of the bridegroom." For the Church is espoused to Christ, the new High Priest, but it was entrusted to the old priesthood, as to a friend who would help prepare the bride to meet her groom. Thus, the Old Covenant sacraments, as well as the baptism of John, were preparatory and intended to lead up to the sacraments, grace, and doctrine of the New Covenant: "John baptized with water, but in a few days you will be baptized with the Holy Spirit."[42] By means of the baptism of John, for example, the people began to be accustomed to the baptism of Jesus. By means of the Passover liturgy, the people were prepared for the new Passover of the Messiah, in which the Messiah Himself would be the Lamb upon whom the participants fed. Indeed, John calls Jesus the Lamb of God, which implies that Jesus is not only the priest but the victim of sacrifice.

Finally, in their public ministries, John instructs the soldiers and tax collectors to do no injustice and refrain from evil, but Jesus teaches them inwardly by His grace to practice divine charity and humility. Thus, the tax collector

---

[42] Acts 1:5. Thus, St. Thomas Aquinas states: "The whole teaching and work of John was preparatory to Christ, just as the ministrations of a subordinate artisan is for the sake of preparing the material for the form which the principal artist introduces" (*ST*, IIIa, q. 38, c.).

Zacchaeus is moved to give half his possessions to the poor, and the centurion proclaims himself unworthy that Jesus should enter under his roof.

In summary, in comparison to the old priesthood, the new priesthood has in itself the source of grace, while the old priesthood only prefigured it; it is more universal; it is holier and capable of causing greater holiness in others; and the new priest is both priest and victim. Perhaps this is one of the reasons why Jesus could say: "among those born of women there has risen no one greater than John the Baptist; yet he who is least in the kingdom of heaven is greater than he."[43] And John, in turn could say: "He must increase, but I must decrease."[44]

St. John: A Patron Saint for Priests

John was a priest living among perhaps the most corrupt priesthood in the history of Israel. Jesus said that the generation of leaders in Israel were so evil that they would be "charged with the blood of all the prophets shed since the foundation of the world, from the blood of Abel to the blood of Zechariah who died between the altar and the temple building."[45] John's response to this corruption is a model for all priests who desire to live a holy life and desire to respond to the corruption of their times.

John did not begin by trying to reform the structures of priestly succession or the worship at the Temple. Instead, he

---

[43] Mt 11:11.
[44] Jn 3:30.
[45] Lk 11:50–51.

went out into the wilderness and prayed and lived a life of penance in union with God. He waited for the Lord to take the initiative regarding how he should publicly respond to the corrupt state of affairs in the priesthood. And while he was there in the desert, the word of the Lord came to him: "the word of God came to John the son of Zechariah in the wilderness."[46] The same word which came to him in the wilderness interiorly would come exteriorly and visibly in the person of Jesus Christ, the Word, only a short time later. It seems that God spoke to John and gave him his instructions just at the time when John would have normally taken up his priestly duties in the Temple (at the age of thirty). But unlike his father, Zechariah, John could no longer minister at the Temple, as was customary for priests. But when he reached the prescribed age to begin his ministry, the Lord gave him instructions about what to do: the Lord sends him to baptize and preach in order to bring people to repentance. John did not have to go to the Temple to offer pleasing worship to God, for all of Jerusalem and Judea went out to him by the Jordan. And the worship he offered, as well as those who were baptized by him, was a humble contrite heart.

St. Norbert of Xanten was a saint dedicated to the reform of the clerical life. In his time, the clergy had become notoriously corrupt. One reading of St. Peter Damien's *Book of Gomorrah* is enough to give a picture of the state of the priesthood in St. Norbert's time. And St. Norbert responded much like John the Baptist. He retired to the wilderness and lived a life of prayer and penance. There he worshipped with

---

[46] Lk 3:2.

his fledgling community in a small chapel dedicated to St. John the Baptist. And the people began to come to him out in the wilderness. His devotion to John the Baptist was not coincidental: St. Norbert saw in St. John a model and patron saint for the priesthood in difficult times. Like St. John, St. Norbert preached against powerful rulers and corrupt clergy. At one point, he even publicly corrected the pope.

In our times, we do well to imitate St. John the Baptist and St. Norbert, and to invoke their intercession. For they offer priests not only a model but an intercessor for the needs of the modern Church. If we, priests and layfolk alike, live a life faithful to God, even if it be on the fringes of the Church, in the wilderness, Christ Himself will come and restore His Church.

Chapter 7

Friend of the Bridegroom

John did not like to talk about himself. When others asked him who he was, he instead told them who he was not. When pressed, he finally admitted that he was a voice of one crying out in the wilderness. However, on one occasion, John volunteered another title for himself. That occasion was when it became known that Jesus's disciples began baptizing, so that everyone began going over to him.

> After this Jesus and his disciples went into the land of Judea; there he remained with them and baptized. John also was baptizing at Aenon near Salim, because there was much water there; and people came and were baptized. For John had not yet been put in prison. Now a discussion arose between John's disciples and a Jew over purifying. And they came to John, and said to him: "Rabbi, he who was with you beyond the Jordan, to whom you bore witness, here he is, baptizing, and all are going to him." John answered: "No one can receive anything except what is given him from heaven. You yourselves bear me witness, that I said, I am not the Christ, but I have been sent before him. He who has the bride is the bridegroom; the friend of

the bridegroom, who stands and hears him, rejoices greatly at the bridegroom's voice; therefore, this joy of mine is now full. He must increase, but I must decrease."[1]

Perhaps lost in the overall theme of John's humility here is the fact that John, without being asked, gives himself a title or a name. He refers to himself as the "friend of the bridegroom." Not only that, he who has simply identified himself as "a voice" mentions that he "rejoices greatly at the bridegroom's voice." The purpose of this chapter is to understand as well as possible what John means by calling himself the friend of the bridegroom.

Bride and Bridegroom in the Old Testament

The authors of the Old Testament often used the metaphor of a spousal relationship between the Lord and His people. However, most of these texts speak of Israel's infidelity and adultery.[2] The text of Jeremiah 3 is particularly poignant:

> If a man divorces his wife and she goes from him and becomes another man's wife, will he return to her? Would not that land be greatly polluted? You have played the harlot with many lovers; and would you return to me? says the Lord. Lift up your eyes to the bare heights, and see! Where have you not been lain with? By the waysides you have sat awaiting lovers like

---

[1] Jn 3:22–30.
[2] See, for example, Deuteronomy 31; Exodus 34; Judges 2; Isaiah 1; Jeremiah 3; Ezekiel 16; Hosea 4–5.

an Arab in the wilderness. You have polluted the land with your vile harlotry. Therefore, the showers have been withheld, and the spring rain has not come; yet you have a harlot's brow, you refuse to be ashamed. Have you not just now called to me, "My father, thou art the friend of my youth-will he be angry forever, will he be indignant to the end?" Behold, you have spoken, but you have done all the evil that you could. The Lord said to me in the days of King Josiah: "Have you seen what she did, that faithless one, Israel, how she went up on every high hill and under every green tree, and there played the harlot? And I thought, 'After she has done all this she will return to me'; but she did not return, and her false sister Judah saw it. She saw that for all the adulteries of that faithless one, Israel, I had sent her away with a decree of divorce; yet her false sister Judah did not fear, but she too went and played the harlot. Because harlotry was so light to her, she polluted the land, committing adultery with stone and tree. Yet for all this her false sister Judah did not return to me with her whole heart, but in pretense," says the Lord. And the Lord said to me, "Faithless Israel has shown herself less guilty than false Judah." Go, and proclaim these words toward the north, and say: "Return, faithless Israel, says the Lord. I will not look on you in anger, for I am merciful, says the Lord; I will not be angry forever."[3]

---

[3] Jer 3:1–12.

Jeremiah speaks of the infidelity of both Israel and Judah, which has largely taken the form of idolatry. The Lord accuses His people of adultery so flagrant that no human husband would take such a wife back to him since it would cause great scandal. Moreover, Israel's repentance is a matter of words alone, without interior conversion of heart: "Behold, you have spoken, but you have done all the evil that you could." And yet the Lord is willing to lower Himself to such an extent that He intends to take His people back even after they have not yet shown signs of true repentance. So while most of the spousal imagery in the Old Testament is condemnatory in tone due to Israel's infidelity, it still reveals a fidelity and love on God's part greater than any human spouse.

Within the context of spousal imagery used in the Old Testament, it is important to distinguish between images which convey a spousal relationship between God and His people and the imagery of bride and bridegroom. The expressions bridegroom and bride not only communicate the notion of a spousal relationship but, more specifically, a young man and woman in the very *act* of being married. For just as there is a great difference between the relationship between a husband and wife over the course of their marriage and the relationship between a bridegroom and bride at the moment they are being married, so also there is a great difference between what is signified by spousal imagery and the imagery of bridegroom and bride in the Old Testament. In some sense, the moment of the wedding stands as a standard or norm against which the whole of someone's marriage is measured. An ideal marriage is one in which husband and wife always relate to one another as they did on their wedding day. Granted, the passions of youth often disguise themselves as deep love, whereas a truer proof of love is a lifetime of fidelity regardless of feelings. Nevertheless, the way in which newlyweds act towards one another always serves as a standard for how spouses should act towards one another throughout their entire marriage.

The prophet Hosea highlights the distinction between a spousal relationship and the relationship between bridegroom and bride when describing Israel's relationship with the Lord when Israel first entered into the Promised Land. "Therefore, behold, I will allure her, and bring her into the wilderness, and speak tenderly to her. And there I will give her her vineyards, and make the Valley of Achor a door of hope. And there she shall answer as in the days of her youth, as at the time when she came out of the land of Egypt. And in that day, says the Lord, you will call me, 'My husband.'"[4]

At this time, the Lord had prepared for Himself a people receptive to His graces and obedient to His will. All those who had previously disobeyed the Lord and distrusted in His mercies had fallen in the desert, leaving only the pure of heart. And so Israel was like a bride: one who responded to her bridegroom's love, and who was willing to form the covenant of marriage. This ideal state of the relationship between Israel and the Lord is depicted more rarely in Scripture; however, the places are notable. Nearly the entirety of the Song of Songs follows this theme, and the prophet Isaiah gives it clear expression: "As the bridegroom rejoices over

---

[4] Hos 2:14–16.

the bride, so shall your God rejoice over you."[5] And we have already seen the text from the prophet Hosea.

John as Friend of the Bridegroom

When, therefore, John describes himself as friend of the bridegroom, he is pointing to the fact that in Christ, the relationship between God and His people will not merely be spousal but bridal. It will be marriage in its ideal state, not marked by any of the defects associated with a bad marriage. Jesus sees Himself as the bridegroom of the Church,[6] as if He is in the very act of being united to the Church in marriage. John, too, is aware of this relationship of Jesus to God's people, and so upon hearing that Jesus has begun to baptize, that is, to wash and sanctify His bride for Himself, John describes himself as the friend of the bridegroom.

It would be tempting for a modern American to hastily identify the "friend of the bridegroom" with what we call today the "best man." There is some warrant to that identification inasmuch as both refer to someone who is the closest friend of the groom and who holds a place of honor at the wedding. But the friend of the bridegroom in Jesus's time and culture was much more than that. The Hebrew word for friend of the bridegroom was *shoshben*, which was the man chosen by the bridegroom to plan and implement all the essentials of the marriage.[7] He invited the guests, planned and organized the wedding ceremony, and hosted

---

[5] Is 62:5.
[6] See Mt 9:15; Mk 2:19–20; Lk 5:34–35; and Mt 25.
[7] See Barrett, CK, *The Gospel According to St. John*. 2nd ed. London: SPCK, 1978 (p. 223).

the reception. He was even charged with the responsibility to locate a new home for the bridegroom and bride. And, therefore, everyone at the wedding answered to the *shoshben*. Most importantly, however, it was the friend of the bridegroom who was the liaison between the bridegroom and bride during the time of the betrothal. Indeed, this aspect of his office continued all the way up until the wedding, where his last and most important responsibility was to protect the bridal chamber.

After the wedding ceremony, it was he who would open the door to the bridal chamber for the bride, and thereafter, he would remain outside the door to prevent any false lovers from entering. It was precisely because he knew the bridegroom so well and recognized his voice so unerringly that the *shoshben* was chosen for this most sacred responsibility. If the bridegroom should come at night, when it would be difficult to recognize his features, the *shoshben* would know the sound of his friend's voice and so be assured of allowing only him who was the true bridegroom to enter the bridal chamber. His office fulfilled, he would then go off to join the wedding banquet with the other guests.

In light of these details, we can see just how important, far-reaching and essential John's role was in preparing for the wedding between Christ and His Church. When the angel Gabriel prophesied about John that he would "make ready for the Lord a prepared people,"[8] this described his role as friend of the bridegroom. John was the liaison between Christ and the Church, readying the Church in every way to

---

[8] Lk 1:17.

become a fit bride for Christ the Bridegroom. John invited the guests by calling them to repentance: "Bear fruits that befit repentance, and do not begin to say to yourselves, 'We have Abraham as our father.'"[9] He prepared the ceremony, anticipating the baptism of Christ: "he went into all the region about the Jordan, preaching a baptism of repentance for the forgiveness of sins."[10] Finally, he protected the bridal chamber; that is, he sanctified the union of marriage by not permitting it to be adulterated by false doctrines about marriage. He did this by opposing the unlawful marriage between Herod and Herodias. This sheds new light upon John's question for the Lord: "Are you he who is to come?" That is, are you the true Bridegroom? Once John recognized the voice of the Bridegroom, he departed this life in joy, just as he had entered it with joy at the voice of the mother of the Bridegroom, she who was herself the bridal chamber of the union of divinity and humanity.

---

[9] Lk 3:8.
[10] Lk 3:3.

Chapter 8

Martyr for Marriage

John's life ended in a manner worthy of its beginning. John offered his life for the sake of the truth he was sent to preach. And just as his birth had been ordained by God, so also his death. From beginning to end, John's life was a life fully guided by and in conformity with God's plan.

The title of this chapter may occasion some reflection: Was John really a martyr? After all, a martyr is one who is killed out of hatred for the faith, the truths revealed by God. But the truth John died for seemed to be a prescription of the Old Law, not really a part of the gospel of Jesus. Is someone who dies to attest that trees are green in the summer a martyr? Is someone who dies rather than eat pork according to the prescriptions of the Old Law a martyr? We shall have to investigate these and similar questions in the pages which follow.

A good place to begin this investigation is the gospel texts which record the death of John. The most detailed text is that taken from the Gospel according to Mark:

> King Herod heard of it; for Jesus' name had become known. Some said, "John the baptizer has been raised from the dead; that is why these powers are at work

in him." But others said, "It is Eli′jah." And others said, "It is a prophet, like one of the prophets of old." But when Herod heard of it he said, "John, whom I beheaded, has been raised." For Herod had sent and seized John, and bound him in prison for the sake of Hero′di-as, his brother Philip's wife; because he had married her. For John said to Herod, "It is not lawful for you to have your brother's wife." And Hero′di-as had a grudge against him, and wanted to kill him. But she could not, for Herod feared John, knowing that he was a righteous and holy man, and kept him safe. When he heard him, he was much perplexed; and yet he heard him gladly. But an opportunity came when Herod on his birthday gave a banquet for his courtiers and officers and the leading men of Galilee. For when Hero′di-as' daughter came in and danced, she pleased Herod and his guests; and the king said to the girl, "Ask me for whatever you wish, and I will grant it." And he vowed to her, "Whatever you ask me, I will give you, even half of my kingdom." And she went out, and said to her mother, "What shall I ask?" And she said, "The head of John the baptizer." And she came in immediately with haste to the king, and asked, saying, "I want you to give me at once the head of John the Baptist on a platter." And the king was exceedingly sorry; but because of his oaths and his guests he did not want to break his word to her. And immediately the king sent a soldier of the guard and gave orders to bring his head. He went and beheaded him in the prison, and brought his head on a platter, and gave it to the girl; and the girl gave it to her mother. When his disciples heard of it, they came and took his body, and laid it in a tomb.[1]

When Herod first heard of Jesus, it was shortly after he had beheaded John. Somehow, Herod believed that Jesus was John raised up. This probably accounts for Herod's intense desire to see Jesus. Even while John was in prison, Herod liked to listen to John. Naturally, it must have been a disappointment for Herod when he finally saw Jesus, and Jesus, unlike John, refused to speak to him. Where did Herod conceive of this possibility that John would be raised up? It is unlikely that he followed the religious debates between the Pharisees and Sadducees. Herod probably took relatively little interest in religion at all. But we do know that he used to listen to John while John was held in custody. So it is reasonable to suppose that John was the one who had told Herod about the resurrection of the dead. And John was so convincing and gave such a powerful witness by his life that, although he performed no miracle, even Herod found John's teaching to be plausible.

If someone were to ask you why John was imprisoned and eventually killed, you might be tempted to say that it was because Herod did not like the fact that John was preaching against his unlawful marriage. But if we read the text more closely, it seems that it was Herodias more than Herod who was offended. Herod imprisoned John "on account of Herodias" who "harbored a grudge against him and wanted to kill him." But it seems that she was prevented in her intention because "Herod feared John, knowing him to be a righteous

---

[1] Mk 6:14–29.

and holy man." In this way, John was very much like his predecessor Elijah, who was persecuted more by Jezebel, the foreign wife of Ahaz, than by Ahaz himself. Both Ahaz and Herod seemed to have some small spark of goodness left in them, which they allowed to be extinguished by the envy of their wives. This is a common theme throughout Scripture: the devil tempts a man through his wife, as he tempted Adam through Eve, Job through his wife, and so on. This shows the importance for a man to have a virtuous wife.

As we continue to read through the account of the death of John, a certain irony becomes apparent. Herodias was angry because John had said it was immoral for Herod to marry his brother's wife. It is obvious that families cannot live together in peace if family members begin to desire one another in a romantic way. The relationships between family members such as brothers and sisters, parents and children, brothers-in-law and sisters-in-law, etc., are incompatible with relationships based upon sexual desire. For if it were permitted for family members to desire one another in this way, the natural jealousies attendant upon romantic love would tear the family apart. John is safeguarding the family, therefore, by preaching about the immorality of a man marrying his brother's wife. But notice that the occasion of the death of John was the promise Herod had made to the daughter of Herodias. Herodias's daughter (who was now simultaneously his niece and stepdaughter!) had so delighted Herod that he swore he would give her even "half of my kingdom." In other words, Herod was proposing that he and the daughter of Herodias together rule the kingdom. That would effectively make Herodias's daughter his new wife.

So here is the great irony: the very principle which John was defending in his preaching was the only thing standing between Herod casting off Herodias in favor of her daughter! Incest is an ugly thing, and its illicit beneficiaries soon become its victims.

It often happens that those who stand to gain the most from the teachings of Christ and His Church are the most vocal opponents to that very teaching. This is nowhere more apparent than in the teachings about marriage and family. It is usually people from broken families who express the greatest outrage over the Church's teaching against divorce and remarriage, the redefinitions of marriage, fornication, adultery, homosexual acts, contraception, and so on. People from intact, happy families experience the benefits of living in a home where chastity and fidelity are practiced, and so they rarely object to the Church's teachings on these things. On the other hand, the very reason why most of those who object to the Church's teachings are themselves victims of broken families is because their family members, especially their parents, refused to abide by the Church's teaching in these areas. And so these unfortunate souls are raised without a loving father and mother in a lifelong communion of life and love. They are victims of the very errors and evils which they seek to defend. But like John the Baptist, the Church and her faithful preachers continue to speak the whole truth so that perhaps a few will be saved.

Proto-Martyr for a Proto-Sacrament

Returning to the question about whether John's death can be considered a martyrdom, notice that John dies not for a ceremonial prescript of the Old Law (like the eating of pork), nor for a statement of fact about the real world (such as the fact that 2+2 makes 4). Instead, John dies for a truth of the moral law: that close family members should not marry one another, or be sexually involved with one another. Notice, too, that there is something about this truth that goes beyond just the natural moral law. For marriage, even under the Old Law, was a kind of proto-sacrament of the union of the divine and the human. Jesus Himself implies this when He defends the indissolubility of marriage by referring to the original union of Adam and Eve by God. Even before the institution of the seven sacraments by Christ, marriage already had the nature of a sacred sign which signified the Incarnation. It was the first sacred sign instituted by God at the origin of our race in paradise when He united Adam and Eve in marriage. St. Thomas says that "before the state of sin, man had explicit faith about the Incarnation of Christ. . . . For the Incarnation of Christ seems to have been foreknown through what was said: 'a man shall leave his father and mother and cling to his wife;'" after which he immediately adds, "It is not credible that the first man was ignorant about this sacrament."[2] Marriage is like John: it straddles the Old and New Covenants and belongs in some way to both. So

---

[2] *ST*, IIa-IIae, q. 2, a. 7, c. Of course, at this point, marriage was not yet a sacrament in the full sense it would later have when Christ raised it to a sign which would communicate grace by His institution.

it is fitting that John should be the one who dies defending marriage. John dies, in some way, for the truth revealed by God, which makes him a martyr in the proper sense.

There is a second consideration about the death of John which manifests that he is truly a martyr—that is, a witness to Christ. John dies because he performs an act of fraternal correction. Consider why John was the one to make this act. To whom did it belong to correct the king? It belongs first and foremost to the one set over the king: God's own representative who speaks on behalf of God Himself. Over and over again in the Old Testament, it falls to God's representative to correct the king. God sends Elijah to correct Ahaz, Nathan to correct David, Samuel to correct Saul, and so on. But John was not the only one who spoke for God at that time: Jesus also spoke on behalf of God, and even more so than John. So why didn't it fall to Jesus rather than to John to correct Herod publicly? John knew that Jesus's hour had not yet come. And so it fell to him to be the voice of the Lord correcting Herod and Herodias. Looked at from this perspective, there is a sense in which John dies for Jesus. This makes it even more plain that John died a martyr's death.

St. John: A Patron Saint for Marriage and Family

From the beginning of John's story, we see the essential connection between his mission and the good of the family. The angel Gabriel prophesied that John would "turn the hearts of the fathers to the children."[3] John's father, Zechariah, had to let go of his own plans for his son, and John would

---

[3] Lk 1:17.

voluntarily sacrifice the joys of family life when, inspired by God, he went out into the desert at a young age. Finally, at the end of his life, John gives his own life to defend the right order of family life as intended by God. John instinctively knew what Jesus would later teach: "He who loves father or mother more than me is not worthy of me; and he who loves son or daughter more than me is not worthy of me."[4] John knew that the love of God above all things was the ultimate foundation upon which happy families must be built. In fact, John understood the family for what it really is: not merely a community for satisfying the needs of nature and human procreation but rather a sign of higher realities, a window into the inner life of God.

And so, the human family is a privileged sign intended by God to lead us into supernatural realities. When we survey the principal mysteries of our faith, we find that they are expressed in terms of relationships within the human family. For example, God is a Father who has an eternally begotten Son. This is the foundational truth of our faith. The relationship of this Son to His Church is that of a bridegroom to his bride. The love of God for His people is like that of a mother for her infant child, and so on.

The Scriptures begin and end with a marriage: the marriage of Adam and Eve in Genesis and the wedding feast of the Lamb in the book of Revelation. Jesus Himself begins His public ministry at the Wedding of Cana, where He manifested His glory and His disciples first began to believe in Him. This is not by chance. The natural beginning of the

---

[4] Mt 10:37.

Christian faith is in the Christian family, and the first sacrament by which children come to believe is the marriage between their parents. For while habitual faith is infused first at baptism, that faith becomes actual through the witness of the sacrament of Matrimony. The sacrament of Matrimony is the first sign by which Christ is glorified, and children first learn to believe in Christ's love for them; they first become disciples through the marriage of their parents. And marriage is not a saving sacrament for the children only but also for all those who shall come into intimate contact with that marriage.

In the beginning of creation, God blessed each day and called it good (see Gn 1). But on one occasion, it was not good: it was not good for the man to be alone. Yet once woman was made from man, God said that it was very good. Every artist has his favorite work of art, and God's favorite is the human family. From all eternity, in fact, He understood Himself as the Son of Mary, as a member of a human family. The reason for God's predilection is that more than the other parts of His creation, the family reflected His own goodness and beauty. Hence, we cannot know God, we cannot love Him, without knowing and loving the natural human family. To do so would be tantamount to considering someone beautiful whose accurate reflection in a mirror we consider ugly.

Because the relationships in a human family are the first (and, in some sense, only) signs by which the fundamental mysteries of the interior life of God are made known to us, it is absolutely essential that these relationships be protected, fostered, and loved. For if these family relationships are distorted, destroyed, or even unappreciated, this will ultimately lead to ignorance and error, indifference, or even animosity toward the entire supernatural order. C. S. Lewis eloquently expressed this view many decades ago when he began to see the attempts to rupture nature from divine revelation:

> One of the ends for which sex was created was to symbolize to us the hidden things of God. One of the functions of human marriage is to express the nature of the union between Christ and the Church. We have no authority to take the living and semitive figures which God has painted on the canvas of our nature and shift them about as if they were mere geometrical figures . . . we are dealing with male and female not merely as facts of nature but as the live and awful shadows of realities utterly beyond our control and largely beyond our direct knowledge. Or rather, we are not dealing with them but (as we shall soon learn if we meddle) they are dealing with us.[5]

Grace not only perfects nature but also builds upon it and, in some sense, is signified by nature. This is why Jesus can use analogies from the natural world (mustard seeds, fig trees, fish, etc.) to teach us about the things of heaven. And, of course, marriage and family are the principal natural realities which Jesus uses to teach us about the inner life of God, the mysteries of the kingdom of heaven.

---

[5] *God in the Dock*, Part II, chapter 11: "Priestesses in the Church?"

Shortly before she died, Sr. Lucia, the last surviving seer of Fatima, wrote a letter to Cardinal Carafa in which she said: "A time will come when the decisive battle between the kingdom of Christ and Satan will be over marriage and the family. And those who will work for the good of the family will experience persecution and tribulation. But do not be afraid, because (Our Lady) has already crushed his head." John was the greatest man born of woman, he was the ultimate perfection that our human nature could produce by way of natural generation. So he stands as a sign of the goodness of human nature and the natural world: the best that a marriage and family could produce. It is, therefore, exceedingly appropriate that John should be, in a special way, the patron of marriage and family. Yet, with all his perfections, the least in the kingdom of heaven was greater than John. Nature was destined to be raised up in Jesus Christ, and without him, it would collapse into oblivion. John knew this, and so he humbled himself and submitted himself to the inscrutable plan of God: He must increase, and I must decrease. In doing this, John represents the perfect response of every natural good before the offer of divine grace: to empty oneself of every natural gift in order to be filled with God. This is the calling of marriage and the human family: not to become something other than it is but to be transformed by God into its true reality. Marriage and family must become perfect signs of the divine life even as it is lived here on earth, just as John became perfectly docile to the divine inspirations. John was the perfect instrument of God, just as the voice is the perfect instrument of the Word.

Epilogue

That All Might Believe through Him

In the prologue to St. John's Gospel, we read this remarkable statement about John the Baptist: "He came for testimony, to bear witness to the light, that all might believe through him."[1] The Gospel teaches us that John's mission was universal, that, in some way, it is through John that all those who are destined to life will come to have faith in Jesus. But what does this mean? Does it mean that all men will come to faith in Jesus by John's witness? St. Paul seems to reject this when he states simply: "Not all men have faith."[2] Does it mean that whoever heard John would eventually believe in Jesus? The Gospel of Luke asserts that not all accepted John's preaching: "All the people and the tax collectors justified God, having been baptized with the baptism of John; but the Pharisees and the lawyers rejected the purpose of God for themselves, not having been baptized by him."[3] Then perhaps the statement that all might believe through John means that everyone who comes to believe in

---

[1] Jn 1:7.
[2] 2 Thes 3:2.
[3] Lk 7:29–30.

Jesus must first believe in John. But this, too, seems false to experience: for there have been many who come to believe in Jesus without having even heard about John.

A good place to look to understand the meaning of this assertion in St. John's Gospel is in the Acts of the Apostles, where it describes how many came to believe in Jesus. First of all, the Acts of the Apostles reports that the baptism of John was very widespread throughout the Mediterranean region. For example, we read that "a Jew named Apollos, a native of Alexandria, came to Ephesus. He was an eloquent man, well versed in the scriptures. He had been instructed in the way of the Lord; and being fervent in spirit, he spoke and taught accurately the things concerning Jesus, though he knew only the baptism of John."[4] Again, when Paul was in Corinth, Paul asked some disciples, "Into what then were you baptized?" They said, "Into John's baptism." So Paul responded, "John baptized with the baptism of repentance, telling the people to believe in the one who was to come after him, that is, Jesus." On hearing this, they were baptized in the name of the Lord Jesus.[5] Those who underwent John's baptism seemed to universally come to faith in Jesus without hesitation. In fact, the Gospel according to John records that Jesus "went away again across the Jordan to the place where John at first baptized, and there he remained. And many came to him; and they said, 'John did no sign, but everything that John said about this man was true.' And many believed in him there."[6] This shows how John's baptism was

---

[4] Acts 18:24–25.
[5] Acts 19:3–5.
[6] Jn 10:40–42.

a preparation for Christ. Well did John prepare the way. St. Thomas expressed this by saying: "The entire teaching and work of John was preparatory to Christ, just as it belongs to a minister and inferior artisan to prepare the matter for a form which the principal artist introduces."[7]

So this is one way in which many came to believe in Jesus through John: those who believed in John and underwent his baptism eventually believed in Jesus. But there seems to be an even more fundamental claim being made by the statement that John came so that "all might believe through him." It is significant that at the beginning of the apostolic preaching, John is mentioned by name, and that every Gospel includes an account of John's preaching. Peter indicates that in some way, the story of Jesus begins from John's baptism when he preaches the gospel to the Gentiles for the first time: "Beginning in Galilee after the baptism of John, how God anointed Jesus."[8] Moreover, one of the essential qualifications for someone to be an apostle was that they had known Jesus from the time of John's baptism: "So one of the men who have accompanied us during all the time that the Lord Jesus went in and out among us, beginning from the baptism of John until the day when he was taken up from us—one of these men must become with us a witness to his resurrection."[9] It is as if Peter is saying that unless someone knew Jesus from the baptism of John, he did not really know *who Jesus was*. Now, since the whole deposit of faith has come down to us through the apostles, and since

---

[7] *ST*, IIIa, q. 38, a. 3, c.
[8] Acts 10:37–38.
[9] Acts 1:21–22.

every apostle had to know Jesus from the baptism of John, it follows that the faith of everyone who eventually comes to believe in Jesus presupposes and depends upon the preaching and baptism of John. Even if some particular believer has not heard of John, nevertheless, if the true faith has been accurately handed down to him, that faith implicitly includes what John preached and did.

John is not just one of the prophets, he is, in some way, the most necessary of all the prophets, the one who prepared the way: that narrow and hard way which leads to life, over which all might come to Jesus. This implies that there is no other way to come to Christ except through the way prepared by John.

Appendix A

Early Christian Writers on John the Baptist

John was such a dominant figure in the early history of Christianity that the bulk of the Gospel writer's efforts were spent arguing that he was not the Christ but only a preparation for Him. This appendix reflects some of the views of the earliest Christian authors on the life and person of St. John the Baptist.

Origen (ca. AD 227)

Origen (born c. AD 185, probably in Alexandria, Egypt— died c. 254, Tyre, Phoenicia [now Ṣūr, Lebanon]) was the most significant Greek theologian of the pre-Nicene Church. Though given to theological and philosophical speculation which sometimes led him into serious errors, he nevertheless contributed greatly to the understanding of Scripture. The following excerpts are taken from his Commentary on the Gospel of St. John.

Are you that prophet? And he answered No. John 1:21 If the law and the prophets were until John, Luke 16:16 what can we say that John was but a prophet? His father Zacharias, indeed, says, filled with the Holy Ghost and prophesying, Luke 1:76 And you, child, shall be called the prophet of the Highest, for you shall go before the Lord to prepare His ways. (One might indeed get past this passage by laying stress on the word called: he is to be called, he is not said to be, a prophet.) And still more weighty is it that the Saviour said to those who considered John to be a prophet, Matthew 11:9 But what did you go out to see? A prophet? Yea, I say unto you, and more than a prophet. The words, Yea, I say unto you, manifestly affirm that John is a prophet, and that is nowhere denied afterwards. If, then, he is said by the Saviour to be not only a prophet but more than a prophet, how is it that when the priests and levites come and ask him, Are you the Prophet? he answers No! On this we must remark that it is not the same thing to say, Are you the Prophet? and Are you a prophet? The distinction between the two expressions has already been observed, when we asked what was the difference between the God and God, and between the Logos and Logos. Now it is written in Deuteronomy, A prophet shall the Lord your God raise up unto you, like me; Him shall you hear, and it shall be that every soul that will not hear that prophet shall be cut off from among His people. There was, therefore, an expectation of one particular prophet having a resemblance to Moses in mediating between God and the people and receiving a new covenant from God to give to those who accepted his teaching; and in the case of each of the prophets, the people of Israel recognized that he was not the person of whom Moses spoke. As, then, they doubted about John, whether he were not the Christ, Luke 3:15 so they doubted whether he could not be the prophet. And there is no wonder that those who doubted about John whether he were the Christ, did not understand that the Christ and the prophet are the same person; their doubt as to John necessarily implied that they were not clear on this point. Now the difference between the prophet and a prophet has escaped the observation of most students; this is the case with Heracleon, who says, in these very words: As, then, John confessed that he was not the Christ, and not even a prophet, nor Elijah. If he interpreted the words before us in such a way, he ought to have examined the various passages to see whether in saying that he is not a prophet nor Elijah he is or is not saying what is true. He devotes no attention, however, to these passages, and in his remaining commentaries he passes over such points without any enquiry. In the sequel, too, his remarks, of which we shall have to speak directly, are very scanty, and do not testify to careful study.[1]

He said, I am the voice of one crying in the wilderness: Make straight the way of the Lord, as said Isaiah the prophet. As He who is peculiarly the Son of God, being no other than the Logos, yet makes use of Logos (reason)—for He was the Logos in the beginning, and was with God, the Logos of God—so John, the servant of that Logos, being, if we take the Scripture to mean what it says, no other than a voice, yet uses his voice to point to the Logos. He, then, understanding in this way the prophecy about himself spoken by Isaiah the prophet, says he is a voice, not crying in the wilderness, but

---

[1] Commentary on John, taken from the *Ante-Nicene Fathers*, Vol. X (T&T Clark).

of one crying in the wilderness, of Him, namely, who stood and cried, John 7:37 If any man thirst, let him come unto Me and drink. He it was, too, who said, Luke 3:4 Prepare the way of the Lord, make His paths straight. Every valley shall be filled and every mountain and hill shall be brought low; and all the crooked shall be made straight. For as we read in Exodus that God said to Moses, Behold I have given you for a God to Pharaoh, and Aaron your brother shall be your prophet; so we are to understand—the cases are at least analogous if not altogether similar—it is with the Word in the beginning, who is God, and with John. For John's voice points to that word and demonstrates it. It is therefore a very appropriate punishment that falls on Zacharias on his saying to the angel, Luke 1:18 Whereby shall I know this? For I am an old man and my wife well stricken in years. For his want of faith with regard to the birth of the voice, he is himself deprived of his voice, as the angel Gabriel says to him, Behold, you shall be silent and not able to speak until the day that these things shall come to pass, because you have not believed my words, which shall be fulfilled in their season. And afterwards when he had asked for a writing tablet and written, His name is John; and they all marveled, he recovered his voice; for his mouth was opened immediately and his tongue, and he spoke, blessing God. We discussed above how it is to be understood that the Logos is the Son of God, and went over the ideas connected with that; and a similar sequence of ideas is to be observed at this point. John came for a witness; he was a man sent from God to bear witness of the light, that all men through him might believe; he was that voice, then, we are to understand, which alone was fitted worthily to announce the Logos. We shall understand this aright if we call to mind what was adduced in our exposition of the texts: That all might believe through Him, and This is he of whom it is written, Behold I send My messenger before your face, who shall prepare your way before you. Matthew 11:10 There is fitness, too, in his being said to be the voice, not of one saying in the wilderness, but of one crying in the wilderness. He who cries, Prepare the way of the Lord, also says it; but he might say it without crying it. But he cries and shouts it, that even those may hear who are at a distance from the speaker, and that even the deaf may understand the greatness of the tidings, since it is announced in a great voice; and he thus brings help, both to those who have departed from God and to those who have lost the acuteness of their hearing. This, too, was the reason why Jesus stood and cried, saying, If any man thirst, let him come unto Me and drink. Hence, too, John 1:15 John bears witness of Him, and cried, saying, Hence also God commands Isaiah to cry, with the voice of one saying, Cry. And I said, What shall I cry? The physical voice we use in prayer need not be great nor startling; even should we not lift up any great cry or shout, God will yet hear us. He says to Moses, Exodus 14:15 Why do you cry unto Me? when Moses had not cried audibly at all. It is not recorded in Exodus that he did so; but Moses had cried mightily to God in prayer with that voice which is heard by God alone. Hence David also says, With my voice I cried unto the Lord, and He heard me. And one who cries in the desert has need of a voice, that the soul which is deprived of God and deserted of truth—and what more dreadful desert is there than a soul deserted of God and of all virtue, since it still goes crookedly and needs instruction—may be exhorted to make straight the way of the Lord. And that way is made straight by the man who, far from copying the serpent's crooked journey; while he who is of the contrary disposition perverts his way. Hence the rebuke directed to a man of this kind and to all who resemble him, Why do you pervert the right ways of the Lord? (Acts 13:10)[2]

St. John Chrysostom (ca. 400)

St. John Chrysostom (born AD 347, Antioch, Syria—died September 14, 407, Comana, Helenopontus) was an early Church Father, biblical interpreter, and archbishop of Constantinople. The zeal and clarity of his preaching, which appealed especially to the common people, earned him the Greek surname meaning "golden-mouthed." His tenure as archbishop was stormy, and he died in exile. He was later declared a doctor of the Church. The following excerpt was taken from one of his homilies.

And as they departed, Jesus began to say unto the multitudes concerning John, What went ye out into the wilderness to see? A reed shaken with the wind? But what went ye out for to see? A man clothed in soft raiment; behold, they that wear soft clothing are in kings' houses. But what went ye out for to see? A prophet? yea, I say unto you, and more than a prophet.

---

[2] Commentary on John, taken from the *Ante-Nicene Fathers*, Vol. X (T&T Clark).

Wherefore He saith, "What went ye out into the wilderness to see?" as though He had said, "Wherefore did ye leave your cities, and your houses, and come together all of you into the wilderness? To see a pitiful and flexible kind of person?" Nay, this were out of all reason, this is not what is indicated by that earnestness, and the concourse of all men unto the wilderness. So much people and so many cities would not have poured themselves out with so great zeal towards the wilderness and the river Jordan at that time, had ye not expected to see some great and marvelous one, one firmer than any rock. Yea, it was not "a reed" surely, that "ye went out to see shaken by the wind:" for the flexible and such as are lightly brought round, and now say one thing, now another, and stand firm in nothing, are most like that.

And see how He omits all wickedness, and mentions this, which then especially haunted them; and removes the suspicion of lightness.

"But what went ye out for to see? a man clothed in soft raiment? Behold, they that wear soft clothing are in kings' houses."

Now His meaning is like this: He was not of himself a waverer; and this ye yourselves showed by your earnestness. Much less could anyone say this, that he was indeed firm, but having made himself a slave to luxury, he afterwards became languid. For among men, some are such as they are of themselves, others become so; for instance, one man is passionate by nature, and another from having fallen into a long illness gets this infirmity. Again, some men are flexible and fickle by nature, while others become so by being slaves to luxury, and by living effeminately. "But John," saith He, "neither was such a character by nature, for neither was it a reed that ye went out to see; nor by giving himself to luxury did he lose the advantage he possessed." For that he did not make himself a slave to luxury, his garb shows, and the wilderness, and the prison. Since, had he been minded to wear soft raiment, he would not have lived in the wilderness, nor in the prison, but in the king's courts: it being in his power, merely by keeping silence, to have enjoyed honor without limit. For since Herod so reverenced him, even when he had rebuked him, and was in chains, much more would he have courted him, had he held his peace. You see, he had indeed given proof of his firmness and fortitude; and how could he justly incur suspicions of that kind?

When therefore as well by the place, as by his garments, and by their concourse unto Him, He had delineated his character, He proceeds to bring in the prophet. For having said, "Why went ye out? To see a prophet? Yea I say unto you, and more than a prophet;" He goes on, "For this is he of whom it is written, Behold, I send my messenger before Thy face, which shall prepare Thy way before Thee." Having before set down the testimony of the Jews, He then applies that of the prophets; or rather, He puts in the first place the sentence of the Jews, which must have been a very strong demonstration, the witness being borne by his enemies; secondly, the man's life; thirdly, His own judgment; fourthly, the prophet; by all means stopping their mouths.

Then lest they should say, "But what if at that time indeed he were such an one, but now is changed?" He added also what follows; his garments, his prison, and together with these the prophecy.

Then having said, that he is greater than a prophet, He signifies also in what he is greater. And in what is he greater? In being near Him that was come. For, "I send," saith He, "my messenger before Thy face;" that is, nigh Thee. For as with kings, they who ride near the chariot, these are more illustrious than the rest, just so John also appears in his course near the advent itself. See how He signified John's excellency by this also; and not even here doth He stop, but adds afterwards His own suffrage as well, saying, "Verily I say unto you, among them that are born of women, there hath not arisen a greater than John the Baptist."

Now what He said is like this: "Woman hath not borne a greater than this man." And His very sentence is indeed sufficient; but if thou art minded to learn from facts also, consider his table, his manner of life, the height of his soul. For he so lived as though he were in heaven: and having got above the necessities of nature, he travelled as it were a new way, spending all his time in hymns and prayers, and holding intercourse with none among men, but with God alone continually. For he did not so much as see any of his fellow-servants, neither was he seen by any one of them; he fed not on milk, he enjoyed not the comfort of bed, or roof, or market, or any other of the things of men; and yet he was at once mild and earnest. Hear, for example, how considerately he reasons with his own disciples, courageously with the people of the Jews, how openly with the king. For this cause He said also, "There hath not risen among them that are born of women a greater than John the Baptist."[3]

---

[3] Homily XXXVII, *Nicene and Post-Nicene Fathers*, Series I, Vol. X (T&T Clark).

St. Augustine (ca. 413)

St. Augustine (born November 13, 354, Tagaste, Numidia [now Souk Ahras, Algeria]—died August 28, 430, Hippo Regius [now Annaba, Algeria]) was the most significant and prolific theologian among the Fathers of the Church. He was bishop of Hippo from 396 to 430. His numerous written works shaped the practice of biblical exegesis and helped lay the foundation for much of medieval and modern Christian thought. He is a doctor of the Church. The following excerpt is taken from one of his homilies.

The Church observes the birth of John as a hallowed event. We have no such commemoration for any other fathers; but it is significant that we celebrate the birthdays of John and of Jesus. This day cannot be passed by. And even if my explanation does not match the dignity of the feast, you may still meditate on it with great depth and profit.

John was born of a woman too old for childbirth; Christ was born of a youthful virgin. The news of John's birth was met with incredulity, and his father was struck dumb. Christ's birth was believed, and he was conceived through faith.

Such is the topic, as I have presented it, for our inquiry and discussion. But as I said before, if I lack either the time or the ability to study the implications of so profound a mystery, the Spirit who speaks within you even when I am not here will teach you better; it is the Spirit whom you contemplate with devotion, whom you have welcomed into your hearts, whose temples you have become.

John, then, appears as the boundary between the two testaments, the old and the new. That he is a sort of boundary the Lord himself bears witness, when he speaks of "the law and the prophets up until John the Baptist." Thus he represents times past and is the herald of the new era to come. As a representative of the past, he is born of aged parents; as a herald of the new era, he is declared to be a prophet while still in his mother's womb. For when yet unborn, he leapt in his mother's womb at the arrival of blessed Mary. In that womb he had already been designated a prophet, even before he was born; it was revealed that he was to be Christ's precursor, before they ever saw one another. These are divine happenings, going beyond the limits of our human frailty. Eventually he is born, he receives his name, his father's tongue is loosened. See how these events reflect reality.

Zechariah is silent and loses his voice until John, the precursor of the Lord, is born and restores his voice. The silence of Zechariah is nothing but the age of prophecy lying hidden, obscured, as it were, and concealed before the preaching of Christ. At John's arrival Zechariah's voice is released, and it becomes clear at the coming of the one who was foretold. The release of Zechariah's voice at the birth of John is a parallel to the rending of the veil at Christ's crucifixion. If John were announcing his own coming, Zechariah's lips would not have been opened. The tongue is loosened because a voice is born.

When John was preaching the Lord's coming he was asked, "Who are you?" And he replied: "I am the voice of one crying in the wilderness." The voice is John, but the Lord "in the beginning was the Word." John was a voice that lasted only for a time; Christ, the Word in the beginning, is eternal.[4]

St. Cyril of Alexandria (ca. 430)

St. Cyril of Alexandria (born c. 375—died June 27, 444) was a theologian and bishop active in the complex doctrinal struggles of the fifth century. He is chiefly known for his defense of the orthodox faith in the Incarnation against Nestorius, declaring Christ to be one divine person having a divine and human nature. He was named a doctor of the Church. The following excerpt is taken from one of his homilies.

"For whom the people, it says, were in expectation, and all reasoned in their hearts of John, whether he were not the Christ, he answered them in the words which we have just read."

They had beheld with admiration the incomparable beauty of John's mode of life: the splendor of his conduct; the unparalleled and surpassing excellence of his piety. For so great and admirable was he, that even the Jewish populace began to conjecture whether he were not himself the Christ, Whom the law had described to them in shadows, and the holy prophets had before proclaimed. Inasmuch therefore as some ventured on this conjecture, he at once cuts away their surmise, declining as a servant the honors due to the Master, and transferring the glory to Him Who transcends all, even to Christ. For he knew that He is faithful unto

---

[4] Sermon 293, as found in the Office of Readings for the Nativity of John the Baptist (June 24th).

those that serve Him. And what he acknowledges is in very deed the truth: for between God and man the distance is immeasurable. "Ye yourselves, there, he says, bear me witness that I said I am not the Christ, but that I am sent before Him." But where shall we find the holy Baptist thus speaking? In the Gospel of John, who has thus spoken concerning him; "And this is the testimony of John when the scribes and Pharisees at Jerusalem sent to ask him whether he were the Christ. And he confessed, and denied not, and said, that I am not the Christ, but am he that is sent before Him." Great therefore and admirable in very deed is the forerunner, who was the dawning before the Savior's meridian splendor, the precursor of the spiritual daylight, beautiful as the morning star, and called of God the Father a torch.[5]

St. Caesarius of Arles (ca. 530)

St. Caesarius of Arles (born c. 470, in the region of Chalon-sur-Saône, Gaul [France]—died 542, Arles) was a leading prelate of Gaul and a celebrated preacher whose opposition to the heresy of Semi-Pelagianism was one of the chief influences on its decline in the sixth century. The following excerpt is taken from one of his homilies.

Today we are celebrating the Nativity of St. John, dearest brethren, something which we read has never been granted to any of the other saints. Only the Nativity of our Lord and that of Blessed John [the Baptist] are celebrated and honored throughout the world. A sterile woman bore the

---

[5] "Holy Fathers in Praise of St. John the Baptist," Orthodox Christianity, July 2, 2016, https://orthochristian.com/95097.html.

latter, a virgin conceived the former; in Elizabeth sterility was overcome, in blessed Mary the method of conception was changed. Elizabeth bore her son by knowing a husband; Mary believed the angel and conceived hers. Elizabeth conceived a man, and so did Mary; but Elizabeth conceived only a man, while Mary conceived both God and man.

What did John want for himself? Why was he interposed? Concerning Whom was he sent ahead? For this reason John was great, and to his greatness even the Savior bears testimony when He says, There has not appeared on earth a man born of woman greater than John the Baptist (Mt 11:11). He surpassed and excelled everyone; he excelled the prophets, he surpassed the patriarchs. Anyone who is born of a woman is inferior to John. Perhaps someone may say: If John is greater than all the sons of women, he is greater than the Savior. Far be it from that. John indeed was born of a woman, but Christ was born of a virgin. The former was brought forth from within a corruptible womb, while the latter was born through the flowering of an undefiled womb. Yet the birth of our Lord is considered along with that of John, so that our Lord may not seem to be outside of the reality of human nature. If John is compared with men, that man surpasses all men; none but the God-man excels him.

John was sent ahead, before God. So great was the excellence in him, so great his grace, that he was considered as the Christ. What, then, did he say concerning Christ? Of his fullness we have all had a share (Jn 1:16). What does this mean, "we all"? The prophets, the patriarchs, the apostles, as many holy people as were sent ahead before the Incarnation or were sent after it, we all have shared in His fullness. We are the vessels, He is the fountain.⁶

St. Bede (ca. 725)

St. Bede (born 672/673, Monkton in Jarrow, Northumbria [Eng.]—died May 25, 735, Jarrow) was a priest and Anglo-Saxon theologian, historian, and chronologist. Raised most of his life in a monastery, he dedicated himself to understanding and explaining Sacred Scripture. One of his most important works was the Ecclesiastical History of the English People. He is a doctor of the Church. The following excerpt is taken from one of his homilies.

As forerunner of our Lord's birth, preaching and death, the blessed John showed in his struggle a goodness worthy of the sight of heaven. In the words of Scripture: *Though in the sight of men he suffered torments, his hope is full of immortality.* We justly commemorate the day of his birth with a joyful celebration, a day which he himself made festive for us through his suffering and which he adorned with the crimson splendour of his own blood. We do rightly revere his memory with joyful hearts, for he stamped with the seal of martyrdom the testimony which he delivered on behalf of our Lord.

There is no doubt that blessed John suffered imprisonment and chains as a witness to our Redeemer, whose forerunner he was, and gave his life for him. His persecutor had demanded not that he should deny Christ, but only that

---

⁶ "Holy Fathers in Praise of St. John the Baptist," Orthodox Christianity, July 2, 2016, https://orthochristian.com/95097.html.

he should keep silent about the truth. Nevertheless, he died for Christ. Does Christ not say: *I am the truth?* Therefore, because John shed his blood for the truth, he surely died for Christ.

Through his birth, preaching and baptizing, he bore witness to the coming birth, preaching and baptism of Christ, and by his own suffering he showed that Christ also would suffer.

Such was the quality and strength of the man who accepted the end of this present life by shedding his blood after the long imprisonment. He preached the freedom of heavenly peace, yet was thrown into irons by ungodly men; he was locked away in the darkness of prison, though he came bearing witness to the Light of life and deserved to be called a bright and shining lamp by that Light itself, which is Christ. John was baptized in his own blood, though he had been privileged to baptize the Redeemer of the world, to hear the voice of the Father above him, and to see the grace of the Holy Spirit descending upon him. But to endure temporal agonies for the sake of the truth was not a heavy burden for such men as John; rather it was easily borne and even desirable, for he knew eternal joy would be his reward.

Since death was ever near at hand through the inescapable necessity of nature, such men considered it a blessing to embrace it and thus gain the reward of eternal life by acknowledging Christ's name. Hence the apostle Paul rightly says: *You have been granted the privilege not only to believe in Christ but also to suffer for his sake.* He tells us why it is Christ's gift that his chosen ones should suffer for him: *The sufferings of this present time are not worthy to be compared with the glory that is to be revealed in us.*[7]

---

[7] Homily 23, as found in the Office of Readings for the Death of John the Baptist (August 29).

Appendix B

Litany of St. John the Baptist

Lord, have mercy on us   Christ, have mercy on us.
Lord, have mercy on us,
   Christ, hear us,   Christ, graciously hear us.
God the Father of heaven,   have mercy on us.
God the Son, Redeemer of
   the World,   have mercy on us.
God the Holy Spirit,   have mercy on us.
Holy Trinity, one God,   have mercy on us.
Holy Mary,   pray for us.
Queen of Prophets,   pray for us.
Queen of Martyrs,   pray for us.
St. John the Baptist,   pray for us.
St. John the Baptist,
   precursor of Christ,   pray for us.
St. John the Baptist, glorious
   forerunner of the
   Sun of Justice,   pray for us.
St. John the Baptist,
   minister of baptism to Jesus,   pray for us.
St. John the Baptist,
   burning and shining lamp
   of the world,   pray for us.

St. John the Baptist, angel of
  purity before thy birth,   pray for us.
St. John the Baptist, special
  friend and favorite of Christ,   pray for us.
St. John the Baptist, heavenly
  contemplative, whose
  element was prayer,   pray for us.
St. John the Baptist,
  intrepid preacher of truth,   pray for us.
St. John the Baptist, voice
  crying in the wilderness,   pray for us.
St. John the Baptist, miracle of
  mortification and penance,   pray for us.
St. John the Baptist, example
  of profound humility,   pray for us.
St. John the Baptist, glorious
  martyr of zeal for
  God's holy law,   pray for us.
St. John the Baptist, gloriously
  fulfilling thy mission,   pray for us.
Lamb of God, who takes
  away the sins of the world,   spare us, O Lord.
Lamb of God, who takes
  away the sins of the world,   hear us, O Lord.
Lamb of God, who takes
  away the sins of the world,   have mercy on us.
Christ, hear us,   Christ, graciously hear us.

V. Pray for us, O glorious St. John the Baptist,
R. That we may be made worthy of the promises of Christ.

Let us pray:
O God, Who hast honored this world by the birth of St. John the Baptist, grant that Thy faithful people may rejoice in the way of eternal salvation, through Jesus Christ Our Lord. Amen.